HIP-HOP
LANGUAGE ARTS
THEMATIC TEXTUAL ANALYSIS

Michael Cirelli and Alan Sitomer

The Classics	**The Contemporaries**
Mark Twain	Jay-Z
Aristotle	Lauryn Hill
Frederick Douglass	Nas
Jane Austen	Kendrick Lamar
Oliver Wendell Holmes	Tupac Shakur
Martin Luther King Jr.	Drake
Gandhi	Afrika Bambaataa
The U.S. Constitution	Chuck D
Philip Vera Cruz	Queen Latifah
Lao-tzu	Jeff Chang
Alice Walker	Lupe Fiasco
Ernest Hemingway	Rakim
Sonia Sotomayor	J. Cole
Junot Díaz	Eminem

Delivering the 5th Element of Hip-Hop to Capable Young Minds

1. B-boying **2.** MC-ing **3.** Graffiti Art **4.** DJ-ing **5. Knowledge**

Note: All work contained herein begins with the smart and effective implementation of standards-based lesson plans that have been constructed around three principles:

1. no profanity **2.** no misogyny **3.** no homophobia

Great vocabulary words to discuss; inappropriate elements to validate in a classroom environment.

Hip-Hop Language Arts: Thematic Textual Analysis
by Michael Cirelli and Alan Sitomer

Street Smart Press produces innovative, dynamic teaching
materials that authentically engage students while simultaneously
equipping educators to meet rigorous, high-level academic objectives.

For a host of free, fantastic resources please visit

StreetSmartPress.com
The home of hip-hop pedagogy.

Copyright © 2015 Street Smart Press

ISBN 978-0-9861546-0-7

All rights reserved

First Edition

Cover and Interior Design: Rico Frederick/Jason Lalor
Street Smart Press
3460 Marron Road, Suite 103-160
Oceanside, CA 92056
For all inquiries please visit *www.StreetSmartPress.com*

Typesetters: Wordzworth.com

We strongly encourage all readers to purchase the full iteration of the included works.

Contents

Standards-Based Literacy Skills Targeted in Unit 3
★ Determining Point of View
★ Inform, Persuade, Entertain: Discovering the Author's Purpose
★ Offering Evidence-Based Opinions
★ Exploring Secondary Purposes
★ Close Reading, Line-by-Line Analysis
★ Analyzing Informational Text
★ Reading Charts and Graphs
★ Analyzing International Voices
★ Writing: Making Claims and Providing Evidence

Standards-Based Literacy Skills Targeted in Unit 4
★ Ascertain the Central Idea
★ Synthesize Texts
★ Cite Details
★ Support Assertions with Textual Evidence
★ Explain Your Reasoning
★ Demonstrate Reading Comprehension
★ Analyze Themes
★ Scrutinize Informational Text
★ Read Charts and Graphs
★ Writing: Making Claims and Providing Evidence

Standards-Based Literacy Skills Targeted in Unit 5
★ Understanding Author's Purpose
★ Deducing Tone and Mood
★ Determining Proper Protocol
★ Exploring Digital Considerations
★ Comprehending Style
★ Providing Evidence-Based Reasoning

- ★ Reading Closely
- ★ Examining Word Choice
- ★ Writing Across Modalities
- ★ Unearthing Meaning
- ★ Strong vs. Weak Arguments
- ★ Writing: Making Claims and Providing Evidence

Standards-Based Literacy Skills Targeted in Unit 6
- ★ Identifying Common Themes Between Disparate Texts
- ★ Providing Textual Evidence to Support Assertions
- ★ Recognizing Compositional Similarities
- ★ Distinguishing Stylistic Differences
- ★ Rendering Opinions
- ★ Providing Evidence-Based Reasoning to Support Assertions
- ★ Reading Closely
- ★ Writing: Making Claims and Providing Evidence

Standard-Based Literacy Skills Targeted in Unit 7
- ★ Identifying Common Themes Between Disparate Texts
- ★ Providing Textual Evidence to Support Assertions
- ★ Recognizing Compositional Similarities
- ★ Distinguishing Stylistic Differences
- ★ Rendering Opinions
- ★ Providing Evidence-Based Reasoning to Support Assertions
- ★ Reading Closely
- ★ Writing: Making Claims and Providing Evidence

Pertinent Research Informing Hip-Hop Pedagogy

*ASCD says that effective reading and writing instruction is anchored in providing the opportunity for students to interpret and compose text about subject areas that they find to be personally meaningful.

*NCTE declares that effective teachers understand the critical importance of adolescents' finding enjoyable texts with which to work and that instruction should center around learners' authentic real-world interests.

*The U.S. Department of Education explicitly advocates that teachers help students build confidence in their ability to comprehend texts by making literacy experiences more relevant to students' interests and everyday life.

*IRA says that effective reading instruction remains at the core of any successful attempt at educational reform.

*The O.R.C. says educators who teach reading and writing skills without addressing student engagement are unlikely to yield substantial improvements. The student who refuses to learn will succeed in that effort. On the other hand, students who are motivated to learn can succeed even in less-than-optimal environments.

*The National Center for Education Statistics says studies show that academic achievement is directly associated with engagement in reading and classroom-related activities and that this association is found to hold true for all racial/ethnic/socioeconomic groups as well as for both gender groups.

*The Department of Justice has documented that the link between academic failure and delinquency, violence, and crime is welded to reading failure and that 85% of juveniles who come in contact with the juvenile court system are functionally illiterate (and more than 70% of inmates in U.S. prisons cannot read above a fourth-grade level).

*The Hip-Hop Center for Research and Teaching at New York University estimates that over three hundred classes on Hip-Hop currently are being offered at colleges and universities throughout the United States and abroad.

*The Latino Alliance for Literacy Advancement asserts that low literacy skills make people more likely to be poor, sick, drug addicted, alcoholic, criminal, and homeless. As the Alliance's executive director puts it, "You name the social ill, literacy is the cure."

For more resources and tools, please visit:

StreetSmartPress.com
The home of hip-hop pedagogy

Hip-Hop Language Arts: An Introduction
by Michael Cirelli and Alan Sitomer

Utilizing hip-hop in the classroom has proven to be a game changer for many students and teachers. Classrooms across the United States from Brooklyn to Oakland, Miami to Philadelphia, Los Angeles to Dallas to Chicago to Baltimore, and on and on have been transformed from atmospheres of chronic underperformance and sleepy disengagement to purposeful, dynamic, high-achieving learning environments characterized by meaningful lessons, engaged young people, and soaring academic aims—all by tapping the proven power of hip-hop pedagogy.

This text has been designed to open a similar doorway for you.

Using hip-hop in the classroom isn't a gimmick or a hook; it's research-based, cutting edge U.S. education that has been recognized as efficacious by the U.S. Department of Education, scores of Ivy League universities, and the most significant group of people—real classroom teachers who work on the front lines in U.S. classrooms each and every day. We've moved away from the early models of hip-hop education that leverages its power, to connect to "more acceptable" areas of study, and have situated hip-hop as a pedagogical centerpiece, because hip-hop is relevant, dynamic, and literary.

As educators, authors, speakers, and professional development specialists who have traveled the country extensively providing literacy solutions for "at-risk" youth, we've written this book to help you attain the outstanding results we ourselves have been able to reap with hard-to-reach students in under-resourced schools, with unsupported teachers. When we intentionally create learning tools for 21st-century students, who are often marginalized and have few opportunities to cultivate their own innate literacies, we are centering their needs and experiences by centering hip-hop pedagogy in the teaching and learning process; not as a hook but as a pedagogical equivalent to traditional subject matter. And because hip-hop is a global cultural movement, the information in this text serves all students.

Our data-driven, proven methodologies have unquestionably raised students' achievement and motivation and their general enjoyment of learning. The power in our text comes from its alignment to students. Because we know that today's youth are apprentices to hip-hop culture from birth, we are speaking to their intrinsic skill sets and further developing their learning through standards-aligned teaching tools.

Of course, all of our work begins with the smart and effective implementation of standards-based lesson plans that have been constructed around three inviolable principles:

1. no profanity

2. no misogyny

3. no homophobia

Great vocabulary words to discuss; terrible elements to validate in a classroom environment.

Hip-Hop Language Arts: Thematic Textual Analysis has been designed to foster a literacy-based instructional environment where passion can meet grit, rigor can meet high expectations, and student engagement can meet fidelity to efficacious academic aims through the core tenets and proven track record of hip-hop pedagogy.

You now hold in your hands immediately usable curricular materials designed to serve the needs of capable but disengaged students. Theory is great, but when the bell rings, we know that teachers need actual lesson plans they can trust. This text is where the rubber meets the road, the needle meets the record, and the classics meet the contemporaries.

Historically, too many of our nation's students have been shamed, belittled, and conveniently categorized as underachievers because they have shown an unwillingness to participate and engage with their school's one-size-fits-all educational materials. Years of classroom experience have taught us that one size never fits all. In fact, one size often fits no one.

Is this a text for every kid in every class you will ever teach? Of course not. But is this a book that might be just the right tool to turn on the lightbulb for a very specific segment of your student population? We believe it is.

And we've poured our hearts into giving you our very best.

Michael Cirelli
Publisher, Street Smart Press

Alan Sitomer
CEO, Street Smart Press

Delivering the 5th Element of Hip-Hop to Capable Young Minds

1. B-boying

2. MC-ing

3. Graffiti Art

4. DJ-ing

5. **Knowledge**

We strongly encourage all readers to purchase the full iteration of the included works.

Essential Question

Is violence ever an appropriate
solution for resolving conflict?

Voices in the unit

Kanye West

Martin Luther King Jr.

Tupac Shakur

Nelson Mandela

Frederick Douglass

Gandhi

Ernest Hemingway

Huey P. Newton

U.S. President Lyndon B. Johnson

Afrika Bambaataa

Eminem

Joell Ortiz

Talib Kweli

Lupe Fiasco

Standards-Based Literacy Skills Targeted

Close Reading

What Is Stated/What Is Inferred

Providing Textual Evidence

Deducing the Meaning of Key Words and Phrases

Compare and Contrast

Ideological Analysis

Vocabulary Interpretation

Writing: Making Claims and Providing Evidence

HIP-HOP INTERPRETATION GUIDE
Question: Is violence ever an appropriate solution for resolving conflict?

Consider the following text:

from "Murder to Excellence" by Kanye West (with Jay-Z)

I'm from the murder capital, where they murder for capital
Heard about at least 3 killings this afternoon
Lookin' at the news like dang I was just with him after school,
No shop class but half the school got a tool,
And *I could die any day* type attitude
Plus his little brother got shot reppin' his avenue
It's time for us to stop and re-define black power
41 souls murdered in 50 hours

1. What does Kanye state about whether violence is an appropriate solution for resolving conflict?

   - Kanye clearly states that he does not believe violence is an appropriate solution for resolving conflict.

2. What specific evidence from the text can you provide to support your claim?

   - Kanye directly says in regard to the violence, "It's time for us to stop."

   - Kanye cites the egregious number of deaths (i.e., 41 souls murdered in 50 hours, I'm from the murder capital).

3. What can you infer about Kanye's beliefs based on his claim about whether violence is an appropriate solution for resolving conflict?

   - We can reasonably infer that Kanye does not believe that violence is an appropriate solution for resolving conflict in his community.

   - We also can infer that Kanye is deeply disturbed by the large number of violent acts in Chicago and feels his community needs to rethink the meaning of materialism, power, and respect.

4. What specific evidence from the text can you provide to support your claim?

   - When Kanye mentions "at least 3 killings this afternoon," he is showing the irrationality/inappropriateness of turning to violence to resolve conflict.

   - When Kanye mentions that half of his school has a tool (gun), he is pointing to the false logic of an eye-for-an-eye mentality.

   - When Kanye asks his community to "stop and re-define," he's inferring that he has already done so and come to the conclusion that violence is NOT the answer.

Vocabulary Interpretation: Deduce the Meaning of Key Words and Phrases

What does Kanye mean when he says...

1. "I'm from the murder capital, where they murder for capital"

   - The first part is an allusion to Chicago, 2014, the murder capital of the United States. The second part, "where they murder for capital," explains that in Chicago some people value money (i.e., capital) more highly than they value another human being's life.

2. "No shop class but half the school got a tool"

   - The word "tool" is slang for a gun. The phrase "half the school got a tool" is therefore an illumination of how prevalent weapons are in the city of Chicago. Furthermore, the "No shop class" phrase is a reference to the lack of educational funding being provided to inner city schools.

HIP-HOP STUDENT WORKSHEET
Question: Is violence ever an appropriate solution for resolving conflict?

Consider the following text:

from "Murder to Excellence" by Kanye West (with Jay-Z)

I'm from the murder capital, where they murder for capital
Heard about at least 3 killings this afternoon
Lookin' at the news like dang I was just with him after school,
No shop class but half the school got a tool,
And *I could die any day* type attitude
Plus his little brother got shot reppin' his avenue
It's time for us to stop and re-define black power
41 souls murdered in 50 hours

1. What does Kanye state about whether violence is an appropriate solution for resolving conflict?

   _____

2. What specific evidence from the text can you provide to support your claim?

   _____

   _____

3. What can you infer about Kanye's beliefs based on his claim about whether violence is an appropriate solution for resolving conflict?

   _____

   _____

   _____

4. What specific evidence from the text can you provide to support your claim?

   _____

   _____

   _____

Vocabulary Interpretation: Deduce the Meaning of Key Words and Phrases

What does Kanye mean when he says...

1. "I'm from the murder capital, where they murder for capital"

   _____

   _____

   _____

2. "No shop class but half the school got a tool"

   _____

   _____

   _____

THE CLASSICS INTERPRETATION GUIDE
Question: Is violence ever an appropriate solution for resolving conflict?

On August 28, 1963, Martin Luther King Jr. spoke the following words in Washington, D.C.:

"[T]here is something that I must say to my people, who stand on the warm threshold which leads into the palace of justice: In the process of gaining our rightful place, we must not be guilty of wrongful deeds. Let us not seek to satisfy our thirst for freedom by drinking from the cup of bitterness and hatred. We must forever conduct our struggle on the high plane of dignity and discipline. We must not allow our creative protest to degenerate into physical violence. Again and again, we must rise to the majestic heights of meeting physical force with soul force."

1. What does Martin Luther King Jr. state about whether violence is an appropriate solution for resolving conflict?

- Martin Luther King Jr. states that violence is not an appropriate solution for resolving conflict.

2. What specific evidence from the text can you provide to support your claim?

- Martin Luther King Jr. specifically says that "[w]e must not allow our creative protest to degenerate into physical violence." He is very clear about this point.

3. What can you infer about Martin Luther King Jr.'s beliefs based on his claim about whether violence is an appropriate solution for resolving conflict?

- We can infer that Martin Luther King Jr. believed that there were paths—different, more appropriate paths—to conflict resolution other than violence, paths he held great faith in.

4. What specific evidence from the text can you provide to support your claim about this inference?

- Martin Luther King Jr.'s reference to "conducting this struggle on the high plane of dignity" and cautioning people to "not seek to satisfy our thirst for freedom by drinking from the cup of bitterness and hatred" support the idea of his belief in finding nonviolent solutions.

Vocabulary Interpretation: Deduce the Meaning of Key Words and Phrases

1. What does Martin Luther King, Jr. mean when he says, "We must forever conduct our struggle on the high plane of dignity and discipline"?

- The "high plane of dignity and discipline" is a reference to Martin Luther King Jr.'s deeply held belief that nonviolence is the only acceptable path his people can take to achieve their quest for true "color blind" justice. The "high plane" also can be interpreted to mean that this is the path God would want his people to choose (Martin Luther King Jr. was also a preacher).

2. Martin Luther King Jr. says, "We must rise to the majestic heights of meeting physical force with soul force." Why does he use the word "majestic" to describe these heights?

- Though his people have been beaten, abused, and oppressed, he believes that replying with a strength of spirit is the most dignified, noble, Godly reaction that can be offered. To him, using soul force is not only the proper response but it's also an undefeatable tactic, because it follows both the path to heaven and the path to inevitable victory. The use of soul force is thus "majestic."

THE CLASSICS STUDENT WORKSHEET
Question: Is violence ever an appropriate solution for resolving conflict?

On August 28, 1963, Dr. Martin Luther King spoke the following words in Washington, D.C.:

"[T]here is something that I must say to my people, who stand on the warm threshold which leads into the palace of justice: In the process of gaining our rightful place, we must not be guilty of wrongful deeds. Let us not seek to satisfy our thirst for freedom by drinking from the cup of bitterness and hatred. We must forever conduct our struggle on the high plane of dignity and discipline. We must not allow our creative protest to degenerate into physical violence. Again and again, we must rise to the majestic heights of meeting physical force with soul force."

1. What does Martin Luther King Jr. state about whether violence is an appropriate solution for resolving conflict?

_____

_____

2. What specific evidence from the text can you provide to support your claim?

_____

_____

3. What can you infer about Martin Luther King Jr.'s beliefs based on his claim about whether violence is an appropriate solution for resolving conflict?

_____

_____

4. What specific evidence from the text can you provide to support your claim?

_____

_____

Vocabulary Interpretation: Deduce the Meaning of Key Words and Phrases

1. What does Martin Luther King Jr. mean when he says, "We must forever conduct our struggle on the high plane of dignity and discipline"?

_____

_____

_____

2. Martin Luther King Jr. says, "We must rise to the majestic heights of meeting physical force with soul force." Why does he use the word "majestic" to describe these heights?

_____

_____

_____

HIP-HOP INTERPRETATION GUIDE
Question: Is violence ever an appropriate solution for resolving conflict?

Consider the following text:

from "Violent" by Tupac Shakur

They claim that I'm violent,
Just cause I refuse to be silent
These hypocrites are havin' fits,
Cause I'm not buyin it, defyin it,
Envious because I will rebel against
Any oppressor—and this is known as self-defense

1. What does Tupac state about whether violence is an appropriate solution for resolving conflict?
   - Tupac states that he believes rebellion is an appropriate response to oppression. Rebellion, of course, implies violence, so an argument can be made that he finds violence to be an appropriate response for resolving conflict. However, he also implies violence does not always have to be physical (i.e., it can take other forms).

2. What specific evidence from the text can you provide to support your claim?
   - Tupac directly says, "I will rebel against any oppressor."
   - Tupac says fighting an oppressor "is known as self-defense" (i.e., a justifiable action).

3. What can be inferred about Tupac's beliefs based on his claim about whether violence is an appropriate solution for resolving conflict?
   - It can inferred that Tupac believes he is being wrongly mislabeled as a violent aggressor when, in fact, he feels he is merely standing up to institutionalized tyranny.
   - It can be inferred that Tupac believes he is a voice for many other oppressed people just like him and that it's his moral duty to speak up.

4. What specific evidence from the text can you provide to support your claim?
   - When Tupac mentions "they claim that I'm violent," he is indicating how the establishment portrays him as being an instigator, because this accusation cleverly turns him into the bad guy, when in fact, his opinion is that he feels he's just doing what he needs to do to defend himself and stand up to oppression.
   - Tupac's mentioning "I refuse to be silent" supports the notion that he believes he has weighed the issue of whether to rebel and speak up or remain silent and decided that as a man, it's his duty to speak the truth about his beliefs.

Vocabulary Interpretation: Deduce the Meaning of Key Words and Phrases

What does Tupac mean when he says…

1. "These hypocrites are havin' fits"
   - Tupac's saying "these hypocrites are havin' fits" is a reference to the irony of being labeled violent by people who have a history of being egregiously violent in physical, political, and socioeconomic ways toward people like him—and the hypocrites (like all hypocrites) are not at all happy ("havin' fits") about being called out by him.

2. "This is known as self-defense"
   - Tupac knows that the law—the U.S. law as well as higher moral law—grants a person the right to self-defense. By referencing the idea of self-defense, he is noting that he did not instigate this conflict but that he also is not going to continue to be tyrannized without standing up for his rights.

HIP-HOP STUDENT WORKSHEET
Question: Is violence ever an appropriate solution for resolving conflict?

Consider the following text:

from "Violent" by Tupac Shakur

They claim that I'm violent,
Just cause I refuse to be silent
These hypocrites are havin' fits,
Cause I'm not buyin it, defyin it,
Envious because I will rebel against
Any oppressor—and this is known as self-defense

1. What does Tupac state about whether violence is an appropriate solution for resolving conflict?

_____

_____

2. What specific evidence from the text can you provide to support your claim?

_____

_____

3. What can you infer about Tupac's beliefs based on his claim about whether violence is an appropriate solution for resolving conflict?

_____

_____

_____

4. What specific evidence from the text can you provide to support your claim?

_____

_____

_____

Vocabulary Interpretation: Deduce the Meaning of Key Words and Phrases

What does Tupac mean when he says...

1. "These hypocrites are havin' fits"

_____

_____

_____

2. "This is known as self-defense"

_____

_____

_____

THE CLASSICS INTERPRETATION GUIDE
Question: Is violence ever an appropriate solution for resolving conflict?

On April 20, 1964, Nelson Mandela spoke the following words at the Palace of Justice in Pretoria, South Africa:

"I do not deny that I planned sabotage. I did not plan it in a spirit of recklessness nor because I have any love of violence. I planned it as a result of a calm and sober assessment of the political situation that had arisen after many years of tyranny, exploitation and oppression of my people by the whites."

1. What does Mandela state about whether violence is an appropriate solution for resolving conflict?

  - Mandela states that he believes violence can be an appropriate solution for resolving conflict.

2. What specific evidence from the text can you provide to support your claim?

  - Mandela states that he thoughtfully planned sabotage as an appropriate solution for resolving conflict—and within the sabotage about which he speaks there is violence.

3. What can be inferred about Mandela's beliefs based on his claim about whether violence is an appropriate solution for resolving conflict?

  - It can be inferred that Mandela had tried other avenues to resolve the conflict and none of them had worked, leaving him (and his people) no other choice but to turn to violence to resolve the conflict.

4. What specific evidence from the text can you provide to support your claim about this inference?

  - Mandela speaks of planning the violence "as a result of a calm and sober assessment of the political situation." His decision did not come, as he mentions, out of a "spirit of recklessness" or a "love of violence" but rather as the de facto answer to "years of tyranny, exploitation and oppression."

Vocabulary Interpretation: Deduce the Meaning of Key Words and Phrases

1. Mandela says, "I planned it [sabotage] as a result of calm and sober assessment." Why does he use the word "sober"?

  - People who participate in violence often do so spontaneously, and violence is often committed in a reactionary, impulsive manner. Mandela chooses the word "sober" because he wants to point out that he was not driven by rashness or out-of-control primal emotions; he thoughtfully chose sabotage in a clear-headed manner because after weighing the situation, he came to believe it was the most intelligent and prudent course of action.

2. Why does Mandela use the phrase "after many years of tyranny, exploitation and oppression" in the text?

  - Mandela points out that there has been many years of tyranny, exploitation, and oppression because it supports his claim that his actions come as a response to a long time of not responding by means of "sabotage." In other words, his people have endured inequity for far too long, and he uses this phrase to support his claim that "enough is now enough" and his actions are justifiable.

THE CLASSICS STUDENT WORKSHEET
Question: Is violence ever an appropriate solution for resolving conflict?

On April 20, 1964, Nelson Mandela spoke the following words at the Palace of Justice in Pretoria, South Africa:

"I do not deny that I planned sabotage. I did not plan it in a spirit of recklessness nor because I have any love of violence. I planned it as a result of a calm and sober assessment of the political situation that had arisen after many years of tyranny, exploitation and oppression of my people by the whites."

1. What does Mandela state about whether violence is an appropriate solution for resolving conflict?

_____

_____

2. What specific evidence from the text can you provide to support your claim?

_____

_____

3. What can you infer about Mandela's beliefs based on his claim about whether violence is an appropriate solution for resolving conflict?

_____

_____

4. What specific evidence from the text can you provide to support your claim?

_____

_____

Vocabulary Interpretation: Deduce the Meaning of Key Words and Phrases

1. Mandela says, "I planned it [sabotage] as a result of calm and sober assessment." Why does Mandela use the word "sober"?

_____

_____

_____

2. Why does Mandela use the phrase "after many years of tyranny, exploitation and oppression" in the text?

_____

_____

_____

VENN DIAGRAM Interpretation Guide

MARTIN LUTHER KING

UNIQUE

Saw violence as an inappropriate solution to conflict resolution

Felt that using violence was not dignified

Believed the path to liberation must not trod down the road of violence

SIMILAR

Both men were leaders of people who were oppressed as a result of the color of their skin

Both men were imprisoned for their activism

Both men were revered for their moral heroism

NELSON MANDELA

UNIQUE

Saw violence as an appropriate solution to conflict resolution

Felt that using violence was not reckless

Believed the path to liberation must trod down the road of violence

VENN DIAGRAM for Hip-Hop

TUPAC SHAKUR

UNIQUE

Suggests that violence is an apropos reply to tyranny

Avoid any allusions to particularly violent events (is vague)

References the intelligence of self-defense

SIMILAR

Both use musical lyrics (rap) to offer social commentary

Both are celebrities in the world of hip-hop

Both address the problems of violence in America

KANYE WEST

UNIQUE

Disdains violence as a tool for conflict resolution

Makes a direct reference to Chicago's egregious gun deaths

Understands but questions self-defense (because it leads to chronic gunfire)

VENN DIAGRAM Student Worksheet

MARTIN **LUTHER KING**

UNIQUE

_____
_____
_____
_____
_____

SIMILAR

_____
_____
_____
_____
_____

NELSON **MANDELA**

UNIQUE

_____
_____
_____
_____
_____

VENN DIAGRAM Hip-Hop Student Worksheet

TUPAC **SHAKUR**

UNIQUE

_____
_____
_____
_____

SIMILAR

_____
_____
_____
_____

KANYE **WEST**

UNIQUE

_____
_____
_____
_____

QUOTE ANALYSIS: A BLEND OF CLASSIC THINKERS INTERPRETATION GUIDE
Question: Is violence ever an appropriate solution for resolving conflict?

"Men are whipped oftenest who are whipped easiest." —FREDERICK DOUGLASS

Do you think Fredrick Douglass would claim that violence is an appropriate solution for resolving conflict? Why or why not?

- The quote indicates that Fredrick Douglass believes using violence to combat violence is the only proper way to respond to an attack because surrender, he posits, will only lead to more violence being brought to the door of the person who too easily submits.

"An eye for an eye will only make the whole world blind." —GANDHI

Do you think Gandhi would claim that violence is an appropriate solution for resolving conflict? Why or why not?

- The quote indicates that Gandhi does not believe that violence is an appropriate solution because it becomes a zero sum game, where everyone eventually loses.

"They wrote in the old days that it's sweet and fitting to die for one's country. But in modern war there's nothing sweet nor fitting in your dying. You'll die like a dog for no good reason." —ERNEST HEMINGWAY

Do you think Hemingway would claim that violence is an appropriate solution for resolving conflict? Why or why not?

- It's hard to say, but the quote holds resonance because many urban young people view themselves as street soldiers for their gangs. As Hemingway points out, although these young people think they are sacrificing for a noble ideal, the truth is that they are often dying for "no good reason."

"I do not think that life will change for the better without an assault on the Establishment, which goes on exploiting the wretched of the earth....We have such a strong desire to live with hope and human dignity that existence without them is impossible. When reactionary forces crush us, we must move against these forces, even at the risk of death. We will have to be driven out with a stick."
—HUEY P. NEWTON

Do you think Huey P. Newton would say that violence is an appropriate solution for resolving conflict? Why or why not?

- The quote indicates that he definitely believes in the idea of attacking the "Establishment" that exploits the weak/low/wretched, with violence as an absolutely justifiable tool in the war against injustice.

"The vote is the most powerful instrument ever devised by man for breaking down injustice."
—U.S. PRESIDENT LYNDON B. JOHNSON

Do you think Lyndon B. Johnson would say that violence is an appropriate solution for resolving conflict? Why or why not?

- The quote indicates that he does not believe violence is the appropriate solution for resolving conflict (with the "Establishment"). In a democracy, Johnson clearly believes in the power of the vote.

QUOTE ANALYSIS: A BLEND OF CLASSIC THINKERS STUDENT WORKSHEET

Question: Is violence ever an appropriate solution for resolving conflict?

"Men are whipped oftenest who are whipped easiest." —FREDERICK DOUGLASS

Do you think Fredrick Douglass would claim that violence is an appropriate solution for resolving conflict? Why or why not?

_____

_____

"An eye for an eye will only make the whole world blind." —GANDHI

Do you think Gandhi would claim that violence is an appropriate solution for resolving conflict? Why or why not?

_____

_____

"They wrote in the old days that it's sweet and fitting to die for one's country. But in modern war there's nothing sweet nor fitting in your dying. You'll die like a dog for no good reason." —ERNEST HEMINGWAY

Do you think Hemingway would claim that violence is an appropriate solution for resolving conflict? Why or why not?

_____

_____

"I do not think that life will change for the better without an assault on the Establishment, which goes on exploiting the wretched of the earth....We have such a strong desire to live with hope and human dignity that existence without them is impossible. When reactionary forces crush us, we must move against these forces, even at the risk of death. We will have to be driven out with a stick."
—HUEY P. NEWTON

Do you think Huey P. Newton would say that violence is an appropriate solution for resolving conflict? Why or why not?

_____

_____

The vote is the most powerful instrument ever devised by man for breaking down injustice.
—PRESIDENT LYNDON B. JOHNSON

Do you think Lyndon B. Johnson would say that violence is an appropriate solution for resolving conflict? Why or why not?

_____

_____

QUOTE ANALYSIS: A BLEND OF HIP-HOP ARTISTS INTERPRETATION GUIDE
Question: Is violence ever an appropriate solution for resolving conflict?

"Hip-cop culture was created to be about peace, love, unity and having fun, in order to help people to get away from the negativity that was plaguing our streets." —AFRIKA BAMBAATAA

Do you think Afrika Bambaataa would claim that violence is an appropriate solution for resolving conflict? Why or why not?

- The quote clearly shows that he does not believe violence is an appropriate solution to conflict resolution (i.e., the "negativity plaguing our streets").

"I don't do black music, I don't do white music, I make fight music, for high school kids."
—EMINEM, "WHO KNEW"

Do you think Eminem would claim that violence is an appropriate solution for resolving conflict? Why or why not?

- His quote makes it obvious that he knows his music foments violence, so it can be reasonably inferred that he probably views violence as an appropriate means of conflict resolution.

See every block got a different crew
This kid I knew got paralyzed cause of his tattoo
And he wasn't in a gang
Just some young punk trying to come up and get a name
Put a bullet in his brain, it's a shame. —JOELL ORTIZ, "LATINO"

Do you think Joell Ortiz would claim that violence is an appropriate solution for resolving conflict? Why or why not?

- By noting the shame of a life lost, it's evident that he would not claim that violence is an appropriate solution for conflict resolution.

Promise I'll always love ya, I love to kiss and hug ya
You and your brother should be looking out for one another
I'm so blessed, man, y'all the reason I got up
Somebody put his hands on you I'm getting locked up —TALIB KWELI, "BLACK GIRL PAIN"

Do you think Talib Kweli would claim that violence is an appropriate solution for resolving conflict? Why or why not?

- The last line of the lyrics shows that Talib Kweli does believe that violence would be an appropriate form of conflict resolution (i.e., he loves his kids so much that if someone hurts them, he'll go to jail for violent retribution).

"I've made violent music. Done violent things. Most my friends are violent. Lived in violent neighborhoods. Seen violence first hand. At a certain point you start to get tired of it. You ask why? Why is it like this? What is causing this? Why is this ok to live like this?" —LUPE FIASCO

Do you think Lupe Fiasco would say that violence is an appropriate solution for resolving conflict? Why or why not?

- Lupe Fiasco's quote shows the maturity of a man who once upon a time did view violence as an appropriate form of conflict resolution but now—after being exposed to too much of it—has begun to question whether there might now be a "better" way.

QUOTE ANALYSIS: A BLEND OF HIP-HOP ARTISTS STUDENT WORKSHEET
Question: Is violence ever an appropriate solution for resolving conflict?

"Hip-cop culture was created to be about peace, love, unity and having fun, in order to help people to get away from the negativity that was plaguing our streets." —AFRIKA BAMBAATAA

Do you think Afrika Bambaataa would claim that violence is an appropriate solution for resolving conflict? Why or why not?

_____

_____

"I don't do black music, I don't do white music, I make fight music, for high school kids."
—EMINEM, "WHO KNEW"

Do you think Eminem would claim that violence is an appropriate solution for resolving conflict? Why or why not?

_____

_____

See every block got a different crew
This kid I knew got paralyzed cause of his tattoo
And he wasn't in a gang
Just some young punk trying to come up and get a name
Put a bullet in his brain, it's a shame. —JOELL ORTIZ, "LATINO"

Do you think Joell Ortiz would claim that violence is an appropriate solution for resolving conflict? Why or why not?

_____

_____

Promise I'll always love ya, I love to kiss and hug ya
You and your brother should be looking out for one another
I'm so blessed, man, y'all the reason I got up
Somebody put his hands on you I'm getting locked up —TALIB KWELI, "BLACK GIRL PAIN"

Do you think Talib Kweli would claim that violence is an appropriate solution for resolving conflict? Why or why not?

_____

_____

"I've made violent music. Done violent things. Most my friends are violent. Lived in violent neighborhoods. Seen violence first hand. At a certain point you start to get tired of it. You ask why? Why is it like this? What is causing this? Why is this ok to live like this?" —LUPE FIASCO

Do you think Lupe Fiasco would say that violence is an appropriate solution for resolving conflict? Why or why not?

_____

_____

OPEN MIC: PUTTING THE QUESTION TO YOU!

*Please answer the question below making sure that you
use textual evidence to support whatever claims(s) you assert.*

In your opinion, is violence an appropriate solution for resolving conflict?

_____

_____

_____

_____

_____

_____

_____

_____

_____

_____

_____

_____

_____

_____

_____

_____

_____

_____

_____

_____

_____

_____

_____

_____

UNIT 2
INTERPRET AND ANALYZE WORD CHOICE

Essential Question

Should hip-hop be banned?

Bill O'Reilly	Oliver Wendell Holmes
Michael Eric Dyson	Lupe Fiasco
C. Delores Tucker	David Banner
Jeff Chang and Dave Zirin	Senator Chris McDaniel
Homeboy Sandman	Philippe Dauman
The U.S. Constitution	Barack Obama

Voices in the unit

Standards-Based Literacy Skills Targeted

Analyzing Vocabulary
Synonyms and Antonyms
Dissecting Author Word Choice
Interpreting Tone
Visualizing Text
Offering Evidence-Based Opinions
Writing: Making Claims and Providing Evidence

INTERPRETATION GUIDE
Question: Should hip-hop be banned?

Consider the following text:

> *"For years, I've been saying that the antisocial lyrics contained in many rap songs and the overall tone of boorish behavior in the hip-hop world is having a destructive influence on many of America's most at-risk children."* —BILL O'REILLY, BEST-SELLING AUTHOR AND HOST OF THE TELEVISION SHOW THE O'REILLY FACTOR

1. Determine the meaning of the word "boorish" in the text.
   - Boorish means crude, bad mannered, and unrefined. It also implies a degree of incivility and vulgarity.

2. Analyze and explain why O'Reilly chose to use this particular word.
   - O'Reilly chose to use the word "boorish" to emphasize his belief about the negative impact hip-hop is having on the lives of young people.

3. What textual evidence can you provide to support the assertion you just made above?
   - O'Reilly cites that there are "antisocial lyrics" in many rap songs (i.e., antisocial lyrics go hand in hand with "boorish" behavior).
   - O'Reilly cites the "destructive influence on many of America's most at-risk children" (i.e., boorish behavior in the hip-hop world translates into hip-hop being a detrimental power holding sway over kids—particularly over poor kids).

4. How does O'Reilly's use of the word "boorish" affect the overall tone of the text?
   - O'Reilly's use of the word "boorish" impacts the tone of the text by casting an unambiguously negative light on hip-hop. By using such a strong, highly disapproving adjective, he leaves little doubt about how he feels in regard to the impact hip-hop has over young people.

Boorish

Provide 3 Synonyms	Provide 3 Antonyms
1. rude	1. refined
2. barbaric	2. sophisticated
3. tasteless	3. cultured

Draw a picture of the word:

Note: Research indicates that drawing pictures of targeted vocabulary words is an activity that supports and enhances the acquisition of language. Drawing pictures can deepen understanding as well as improve recall and is well regarded as an excellent pedagogical tool to build academic vocabulary and increase reading comprehension. Why? Because reading, in many ways, is seeing (with the mind's eye). Remember, learners do not need to be Picasso or Dondi to participate and/ or benefit. Stick figures are ok.

STUDENT WORKSHEET
Question: Should hip-hop be banned?

Consider the following text:

"For years, I've been saying that the antisocial lyrics contained in many rap songs and the overall tone of boorish behavior in the hip-hop world is having a destructive influence on many of America's most at-risk children." —BILL O'REILLY, BEST-SELLING AUTHOR AND HOST OF THE TELEVISION SHOW THE O'REILLY FACTOR

1. Determine the meaning of the word "boorish" in the text.

_____

_____

2. Analyze and explain why O'Reilly chose to use this particular word.

_____

_____

3. What textual evidence can you provide to support the assertion you just made above?

_____

_____

_____

_____

4. How does O'Reilly's use of the word "boorish" affect the overall tone of the text?

_____

_____

_____

Boorish

Provide 3 Synonyms	Provide 3 Antonyms
1.	1.
2.	2.
3.	3.

Draw a picture of the word:

INTERPRETATION GUIDE
Question: Should hip-hop be banned?

Consider the following text:

"Does hip-hop degrade society? Do you know crime has declined dramatically in the last 20 years? Murders are down. Assaults are down. Robberies are down... There is no one-to-one correlation between a hip-hop lyric and a subsequent material condition that leads to criminality. That's a mythology."
—MICHAEL ERIC DYSON (2012)

1. Determine the meaning of the word "mythology" in the text.
   - Mythology means untrue and unrelated to actual facts in the text.

2. Analyze and explain why Dyson chose to use this particular word.
   - Dyson chose to use the word "mythology" to emphasize his belief that the perception of hip-hop's negative influence and the reality of hip-hop's actual influence on society are two entirely different things (i.e., they are fiction based).

3. What textual evidence can you provide to support the assertion you just made above?
   - Dyson cites that over the course of the past 20 years (when hip-hop truly went mainstream), the data proves that "Murders are down. Assaults are down. Robberies are down. Rapes are down." Therefore, how can hip-hop cause more crime when crime is actually down as hip-hop grew in popularity?

4. How does Dyson's use of the word "mythology" affect the overall tone of the text?
   - Dyson's use of the word "mythology" impacts the tone of the text by authoritatively putting an exclamation point at the end of the argument he offers. The declarative sentiment expressed in "That's a mythology" sums up his position that the actual facts about the situation do not support the argument that hip-hop has, in any way, a "one-to-one correlation" with criminality.

Mythology

Provide 3 Synonyms	Provide 3 Antonyms
1. folktales	1. reality
2. stories	2. truth
3. legends	3. actuality

Draw a picture of the word:

Note: Research indicates that drawing pictures of targeted vocabulary words is an activity that supports and enhances the acquisition of language. Drawing pictures can deepen understanding as well as improve recall and is well regarded as an excellent pedagogical tool to build academic vocabulary and increase reading comprehension. Why? Because reading, in many ways, is seeing (with the mind's eye). Remember, learners do not need to be Picasso or Dondi to participate and/ or benefit. Stick figures are ok.

STUDENT WORKSHEET

Question: Should hip-hop be banned?

Consider the following text:

> *"Does hip-hop degrade society? Do you know crime has declined dramatically in the last 20 years? Murders are down. Assaults are down. Robberies are down.... There is no one-to-one correlation between a hip-hop lyric and a subsequent material condition that leads to criminality. That's a mythology."*
> —MICHAEL ERIC DYSON (2012)

1. Determine the meaning of the word "mythology" in the text.

_____

_____

2. Analyze and explain why Dyson chose to use this particular word.

_____

_____

3. What textual evidence can you provide to support the assertion you just made above?

_____

_____

_____

4. How does Dyson's use of the word "mythology" affect the overall tone of the text?

_____

_____

_____

_____

Mythology

Provide 3 Synonyms	Provide 3 Antonyms
1.	1.
2.	2.
3.	3.

Draw a picture of the word:

INTERPRETATION GUIDE

Question: Should hip-hop be banned?

Consider the following text:

> *"Because this smut is in the hands of our children, it coerces, influences, encourages and motivates our youth to commit violent behavior—to use drugs and abuse women.... This kind of entertainment should not be protected by the First Amendment. It's obscene, and those protections should not even apply.... It is our moral responsibility to halt the sale of gangsta rap."*
> —C. DELORES TUCKER, HEAD OF THE NATIONAL POLITICAL CONGRESS OF BLACK WOMEN

1. Determine the meaning of the word "coerces" in the text.
   - In the text, the word "coerces" means to persuade, to cause or to unduly pressure.

2. Analyze and explain why Tucker chose to use this particular word.
   - Tucker chose to use the word "coerces" to underscore her belief that naive kids are engaging in antisocial behavior as a result of listening to hip-hop music (i.e., hip-hop pushes them—against their will—down the road of illegal, amoral behavior.

3. What textual evidence can you provide to support the assertion you just made above?
   - Tucker specifically claims that hip-hop "influences, encourages and motivates our youth to commit violent behavior."
   - Tucker claims hip-hop music advocates that children "use drugs and abuse women."

4. How does Tucker's use of the word "coerces" affect the overall tone of the text?
   - Tucker's use of the word "coerces" impacts the tone of the text in a powerful manner because the word makes it seem as if committing violence, using drugs, and being involved in pornography are the automatic by-products that befall children who listen to hip-hop. The word "coerces" implies that if it were not for hip-hop's horrible influence on children, they would not be led astray down these amoral roads.

Coerce

Provide 3 Synonyms	Provide 3 Antonyms
1. compel	1. discourage
2. bully	2. leave alone
3. put pressure on	3. impede

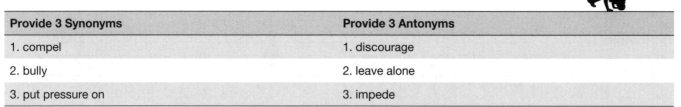

Draw a picture of the word:

Note: Research indicates that drawing pictures of targeted vocabulary words is an activity that supports and enhances the acquisition of language. Drawing pictures can deepen understanding as well as improve recall and is well regarded as an excellent pedagogical tool to build academic vocabulary and increase reading comprehension. Why? Because reading, in many ways, is seeing (with the mind's eye). Remember, learners do not need to be Picasso or Dondi to participate and/ or benefit. Stick figures are ok.

STUDENT WORKSHEET
Question: Should hip-hop be banned?

Consider the following text:

"Because this smut is in the hands of our children, it coerces, influences, encourages and motivates our youth to commit violent behavior—to use drugs and abuse women.... This kind of entertainment should not be protected by the First Amendment. It's obscene, and those protections should not even apply.... It is our moral responsibility to halt the sale of gangsta rap."
—C. DELORES TUCKER, HEAD OF THE NATIONAL POLITICAL CONGRESS OF BLACK WOMEN

1. Determine the meaning of the word "coerces" in the text.

_____

2. Analyze and explain why Tucker chose to use this particular word.

_____

_____

_____

3. What textual evidence can you provide to support the assertion you just made above?

_____

_____

4. How does Tucker's use of the word "coerces" affect the overall tone of the text?

_____

_____

_____

_____

Coerce

Provide 3 Synonyms	Provide 3 Antonyms
1.	1.
2.	2.
3.	3.

Draw a picture of the word:

INTERPRETATION GUIDE
Question: Should hip-hop be banned?

Consider the following text:

> *"The current national monologue about demeaning language and imagery is an exercise in scapegoating. What's being challenged here? Not the media monopolies that twist the proud art form built by artists like Public Enemy, Rakim and The Roots into an orgy of materialism, violence and misogyny. Not the CEOs who aggressively market demeaning music. Not the radio stations that play the same sexist drivel. They are the ones who need to be held to account."*
> —JEFF CHANG AND DAVE ZIRIN, "HIP-HOP'S E-Z SCAPEGOATS," THE NATION

1. Determine the meaning of the word "scapegoating" in the text.

- In the text, the word "scapegoating" means to falsely blame and/or put the blame of something on the wrong people, thing, or culture (i.e., hip-hop culture).

2. Analyze and explain why Chang and Zirin chose to use this particular word.

- Chang and Zirin chose to use the word "scapegoating" to underscore their belief that hip-hop (and hip-hop artists) are being blamed for the negative values (i.e., "demeaning language and imagery") that is found in mainstream hip-hop music.

3. What textual evidence can you provide to support the assertion you just made above?

- Chang and Zirin specifically claim that there is no critical dialogue to "challenge" some of the contributing factors to the promotion of "demeaning language and imagery."
- Chang and Zirin claim that "media monopolies," "CEOs," and "radio stations" are also responsible for promoting music that glorifies "materialism, violence and misogyny."

4. How does Chang and Zirin's use of the word "scapegoating" affect the tone of the text?

- Chang and Zirin's use of the word "scapegoating" impacts the tone of the text in a powerful manner because the word is used to show that all of hip-hop is blamed for the negative language, values, and imagery that appear in some of the music. They decisively make a case for the myriad other entities that are responsible for perpetuating much of the violence and misogyny that we hear in the mainstream hip-hop music media.

Scapegoat

Provide 3 Synonyms	Provide 3 Antonyms
1. blame	1. absolve
2. fool	2. trust
3. mark	3. justify

Draw a picture of the word:

Note: Research indicates that drawing pictures of targeted vocabulary words is an activity that supports and enhances the acquisition of language. Drawing pictures can deepen understanding as well as improve recall and is well regarded as an excellent pedagogical tool to build academic vocabulary and increase reading comprehension. Why? Because reading, in many ways, is seeing (with the mind's eye). Remember, learners do not need to be Picasso or Dondi to participate and/or benefit. Stick figures are ok.

STUDENT WORKSHEET
Question: Should hip-hop be banned?

Consider the following text:

> *"The current national monologue about demeaning language and imagery is an exercise in scapegoating. What's being challenged here? Not the media monopolies that twist the proud art form built by artists like Public Enemy, Rakim and The Roots into an orgy of materialism, violence and misogyny. Not the CEOs who aggressively market demeaning music. Not the radio stations that play the same sexist drivel. They are the ones who need to be held to account."*
> —JEFF CHANG AND DAVE ZIRIN, "HIP-HOP'S E-Z SCAPEGOATS," THE NATION

1. Determine the meaning of the word "scapegoating" in the text.

_____

_____

2. Analyze and explain why Chang and Zirin chose to use this particular word.

_____

_____

3. What textual evidence can you provide to support the assertion you just made above?

_____

_____

_____

4. How does Chang and Zirin's use of the word "scapegoating" affect the overall tone of the text?

_____

_____

_____

Scapegoat

Provide 3 Synonyms	Provide 3 Antonyms
1.	1.
2.	2.
3.	3.

Draw a picture of the word:

INTERPRETATION GUIDE
Question: Should hip-hop be banned?

Consider the following text:

"While alcohol and technology and car brands that advertise through hip hop are raking in the dough, kids in classrooms in New York and New Jersey and across the country are paying the price. They can only think about certain things. They can't be creative. They're ridiculed for breaking rank. For thinking freely. For being different.... Young people today get the majority of their knowledge today from the media they consume, and fans of hip hop just can't fathom the idea that all of the uniformity might be part of a ploy carried out by gigantic corporations seeking to turn everyone into mindless consuming drones."
—HOMEBOY SANDMAN, "ATTACK OF THE CLONES: HOW LACK OF TOPICAL DIVERSITY IS KILLING HIP-HOP AND ITS LISTENERS," THE HUFFINGTON POST

1. Determine the meaning of the word "fathom" in the text.
   - In the text, the word "fathom" means to comprehend and/or understand; therefore, if kids in U.S. classrooms "can't fathom," then Homeboy Sandman is claiming that they can't understand the ploy being executed upon them by gigantic corporations.

2. Analyze and explain why Homeboy Sandman chose to use this particular word.
   - Homeboy Sandman chose to use the word "fathom" to underscore his belief that fans of hip-hop may not understand (or believe) that they are being fooled, marketed to, and dumbed down by "gigantic corporations."

3. What textual evidence can you provide to support the assertion you just made above?
   - Homeboy Sandman specifically claims that "alcohol and technology and car brands" are advertising through hip-hop and that kids/students are paying the price.
   - Homeboy Sandman claims that "vulnerable" students are becoming uniform consumers because they get a majority of their knowledge from media/hip-hop.

4. How does Homeboy Sandman's use of the word "fathom" affect the overall tone of the text?
   - Homeboy Sandman's use of the word "fathom" impacts the tone of the text in a powerful manner because the word is used to show that fans of hip-hop are oblivious to the market forces (i.e., gigantic corporations) that are affecting the knowledge they consume and the music they celebrate. "Fathom" is used to underscore how unbelievable this idea may be to many fans of hip-hop.

Fathom

Provide 3 Synonyms	Provide 3 Antonyms
1. comprehend	1. misunderstand
2. understand	2. fail
3. believe	3. confuse

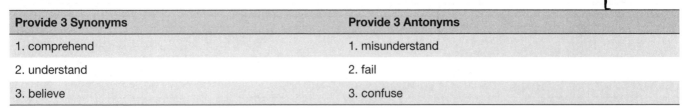

Draw a picture of the word:

Note: Research indicates that drawing pictures of targeted vocabulary words is an activity that supports and enhances the acquisition of language. Drawing pictures can deepen understanding as well as improve recall and is well regarded as an excellent pedagogical tool to build academic vocabulary and increase reading comprehension. Why? Because reading, in many ways, is seeing (with the mind's eye). Remember, learners do not need to be Picasso or Dondi to participate and/ or benefit. Stick figures are ok.

STUDENT WORKSHEET
Question: Should hip-hop be banned?

Consider the following text:

> *"While alcohol and technology and car brands that advertise through hip hop are raking in the dough, kids in classrooms in New York and New Jersey and across the country are paying the price. They can only think about certain things. They can't be creative. They're ridiculed for breaking rank. For thinking freely. For being different.... Young people today get the majority of their knowledge today from the media they consume, and fans of hip hop just can't fathom the idea that all of the uniformity might be part of a ploy carried out by gigantic corporations seeking to turn everyone into mindless consuming drones."*
> —HOMEBOY SANDMAN, "ATTACK OF THE CLONES: HOW LACK OF TOPICAL DIVERSITY IS KILLING HIP-HOP AND ITS LISTENERS," THE HUFFINGTON POST

1. Determine the meaning of the word "fathom" in the text.

_____

_____

2. Analyze and explain why Homeboy Sandman chose to use this particular word.

_____

_____

3. What textual evidence can you provide to support the assertion you just made above?

_____

_____

_____

4. How does Homeboy Sandman's use of the word "fathom" affect the overall tone of the text?

_____

_____

_____

Fathom

Provide 3 Synonyms	Provide 3 Antonyms
1.	1.
2.	2.
3.	3.

Draw a picture of the word:

INTERPRETATION GUIDE
Question: Should hip-hop be banned?

The First Amendment of the U.S. Constitution

"Congress shall make no law respecting an establishment of religion, or prohibiting the free exercise thereof; or abridging the freedom of speech, or of the press; or the right of the people peaceably to assemble, and to petition the Government for a redress of grievances."

1. Determine the meaning of the word "abridging" in the text.

- In the text, the word "abridging" means to shorten, alter, or cut.

2. Analyze and explain why the Founding Fathers chose to use this particular word.

- The Founding Fathers chose to use the word "abridging" to make sure that the Congress would have no right to shorten, modify, cut, or alter anything that a U.S. citizen might seek to say.

3. What textual evidence can you provide to support the assertion you just made above?

- The Founding Fathers' insistence on "freedom of speech" provides the textual evidence needed to support the assertion above. Freedom of speech literally means giving the citizens the right to speak without restraint. To abridge would be to restrain, and the Founding Fathers felt that to give Congress the power to alter anyone's speech by even as little as one word was, in their eyes, too much.

4. How does the Founding Fathers' use of the word "abridging" affect the overall tone of the text?

- The Founding Fathers' use of the word "abridging" greatly impacts the tone of the text because it is such a precise, definite word. When the Founding Fathers deny Congress the right to abridge speech in any manner, their intent is clear and the law of the land is absolute. The word gives the entire text an authoritative, commanding tone.

Abridging

Provide 3 Synonyms	Provide 3 Antonyms
1. lessen	1. expand
2. reduce	2. increase
3. snip	3. enlarge

Draw a picture of the word:

Note: Research indicates that drawing pictures of targeted vocabulary words is an activity that supports and enhances the acquisition of language. Drawing pictures can deepen understanding as well as improve recall and is well regarded as an excellent pedagogical tool to build academic vocabulary and increase reading comprehension. Why? Because reading, in many ways, is seeing (with the mind's eye). Remember, learners do not need to be Picasso or Dondi to participate and/ or benefit. Stick figures are ok.

STUDENT WORKSHEET
Question: Should hip-hop be banned?

The First Amendment of the U.S. Constitution

"Congress shall make no law respecting an establishment of religion, or prohibiting the free exercise thereof; or abridging the freedom of speech, or of the press; or the right of the people peaceably to assemble, and to petition the Government for a redress of grievances."

1. Determine the meaning of the word "abridging" in the text.

_____

2. Analyze and explain why the Founding Fathers chose to use this particular word.

_____

_____

3. What textual evidence can you provide to support the assertion you just made above?

_____

_____

_____

_____

4. How does the Founding Fathers' use of the word "abridging" affect the overall tone of the text?

_____

_____

_____

_____

Abridging

Provide 3 Synonyms	Provide 3 Antonyms
1.	1.
2.	2.
3.	3.

Draw a picture of the word:

INTERPRETATION GUIDE
Question: Should hip-hop be banned?

The Supreme Court also ruled that Freedom of Speech has limitations.

Justice Oliver Wendell Holmes determined there were times when the government could legally restrict speech. To distinguish when Congress could "abridge" a citizen's speech, he formulated the "clear and present danger" test. He wrote:

"The question in every case is whether the words used are used in such circumstances and are of such a nature as to create a clear and present danger that they will bring about the substantive evils that Congress has a right to prevent."

In the case of *Schenck v. United States*, 249 U.S. 47 (1919), the Supreme Court ruled that freedom of speech **does not include the right to incite actions that would harm others** (e.g., shouting "fire" in a crowded theater).

1. Determine the meaning of the word "incite" in the text.
- In the text, the word "incite" means to provoke or instigate.

2. Analyze and explain why Justice Holmes chose to use this particular word.
- Justice Holmes chose to use the word "incite" to make sure that the Congress would have the right to punish those who used words in a manner that could directly cause harm to American citizens.

3. What textual evidence can you provide to support the assertion you just made above?
- In the example given (e.g., Shouting "fire" in a crowded theater), Justice Holmes shows how and why freedom of speech requires limitations. As the Supreme Court points out, to shout fire in a crowded theater when there is no actual fire could create panic and a stampede, and people could be needlessly hurt or trampled. Words, therefore, can become a tool for harm (i.e., the word "fire" being shouted would have incited action that caused injury to the innocent). For this reason Justice Holmes believed freedom of speech required limitations.

4. How does Justice Holmes's use of the word "incite" affect the overall tone of the text?
- Justice Holmes's use of the word "incite" affects the overall tone of the text in two ways. First, it offers clarity. If words directly trigger behavior harmful to others (i.e., if they incite harmful action), they are not protected by the First Amendment. If words do not incite harmful action, then they are covered. Second, the word "incite" affects the tone of the text by bringing conciseness to the ruling. Justice Holmes does not go on and on about what words can and cannot be protected; he tersely defines the limits around speech that "incite actions that would harm others." It's brief and to the point.

Incite

Provide 3 Synonyms	Provide 3 Antonyms
1. encourage	1. prevent
2. trigger	2. tranquilize
3. prompt	3. soothe

Draw a picture of the word:

Note: Research indicates that drawing pictures of targeted vocabulary words is an activity that supports and enhances the acquisition of language. Drawing pictures can deepen understanding as well as improve recall and is well regarded as an excellent pedagogical tool to build academic vocabulary and increase reading comprehension. Why? Because reading, in many ways, is seeing (with the mind's eye). Remember, learners do not need to be Picasso or Dondi to participate and/ or benefit. Stick figures are ok.

STUDENT WORKSHEET
Question: Should hip-hop be banned?

The Supreme Court also ruled that Freedom of Speech has limitations.

Justice Oliver Wendell Holmes determined there were times when the government could legally restrict speech. To distinguish when Congress could "abridge" a citizen's speech, he formulated the "clear and present danger" test. He wrote:

"The question in every case is whether the words used are used in such circumstances and are of such a nature as to create a clear and present danger that they will bring about the substantive evils that Congress has a right to prevent."

In the case of *Schenck v. United States*, 249 U.S. 47 (1919), the Supreme Court ruled that freedom of speech **does not include the right to incite actions that would harm others** (e.g., shouting "fire" in a crowded theater).

1. Determine the meaning of the word "incite" in the text.

_____

2. Analyze and explain why Justice Holmes chose to use this particular word.

_____

_____

3. What textual evidence can you provide to support the assertion you just made above?

_____

_____

_____

4. How does Justice Holmes's use of the word "incite" affect the overall tone of the text?

_____

_____

_____

_____

Incite

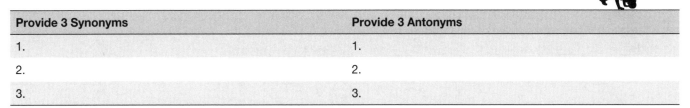

Provide 3 Synonyms	Provide 3 Antonyms
1.	1.
2.	2.
3.	3.

Draw a picture of the word:

INTERPRETATION GUIDE
Question: Should hip-hop be banned?

Consider the following text:

> *"Does violence in music promote/cause/support/influence violence in the world and society? Of course it does. Violent music (and all violent media) effectively says its 'ok' to be violent. It provides positive reinforcement for negative actions. If you rap and make violent music then own up to it. Stop hiding behind 'art imitating life' as a way to evade the guilt."* —LUPE FIASCO

1. Determine the meaning of the word "evade" in the text.

- In the text, the word "evade" means to try to escape the truth of the matter, to avoid feeling bad.

2. Analyze and explain why Lupe Fiasco chose to use this particular word.

- Lupe Fiasco chose to use the word "evade" to clearly make the point that he believes violent lyrics clearly inspire violent behavior. Though he does not speak to the degree to which one leads to the other, he uses the word "evade" to specifically address the motives behind why "deniers" try to use the shield of "art imitates life" (i.e., to avoid or ameliorate their guilt for producing this type of content).

3. What textual evidence can you provide to support the assertion you just made above?

- Lupe Fiasco specifically notes that artists (or media creators) that create violent content must "own up to it" (the "it" being the responsibility of having nurtured, advocated, or perhaps even inspired societal violence).
- Lupe Fiasco notes that "art imitating life" is just an excuse that violent content creators hide behind to avoid owning any responsibility for the consequences of the violent materials.

4. How does Lupe Fiasco's use of the word "evade" affect the overall tone of the text?

- Lupe Fiasco's use of the word "evade" affects the tone of the text in a powerful manner because the word is used in a direct, no-nonsense, almost accusatory manner. Fiasco doesn't make the case that violent material ought not to be published; he's making the point that the publication of violent material incites violence (at some level) and it's cowardly not to own up to this very real by-product.

Evade

Provide 3 Synonyms Provide 3 Antonyms

Provide 3 Synonyms	Provide 3 Antonyms
1. dodge	1. confront
2. elude	2. face
3. avoid	3. tell the truth

Draw a picture of the word:

Note: Research indicates that drawing pictures of targeted vocabulary words is an activity that supports and enhances the acquisition of language. Drawing pictures can deepen understanding as well as improve recall and is well regarded as an excellent pedagogical tool to build academic vocabulary and increase reading comprehension. Why? Because reading, in many ways, is seeing (with the mind's eye). Remember, learners do not need to be Picasso or Dondi to participate and/ or benefit. Stick figures are ok.

STUDENT WORKSHEET
Question: Should hip-hop be banned?

Consider the following text:

> *"Does violence in music promote/cause/support/influence violence in the world and society? Of course it does. Violent music (and all violent media) effectively says its 'ok' to be violent. It provides positive reinforcement for negative actions. If you rap and make violent music then own up to it. Stop hiding behind 'art imitating life' as a way to evade the guilt."* —LUPE FIASCO

1. Determine the meaning of the word "evade" in the text.

_____

2. Analyze and explain why Lupe Fiasco chose to use this particular word.

_____

_____

_____

3. What textual evidence can you provide to support the assertion you just made above?

_____

_____

_____

4. How does Lupe Fiasco's use of the word "evade" affect the overall tone of the text?

_____

_____

_____

_____

Evade

Provide 3 Synonyms	Provide 3 Antonyms
1.	1.
2.	2.
3.	3.

Draw a picture of the word:

MORE VOICES
Question: Should hip-hop be banned?

Do you agree or disagree with the sentiment being expressed in each of the following quotes? Explain by using a segment of the text to support your assertion.

"If by some stroke of the pen hip-hop was silenced, the issues would still be present in our communities. Drugs, violence, sexism and the criminal element were around long before hip-hop existed."
—DAVID BANNER

_____

_____

_____

"Name a redeeming quality of hip-hop. I want to know anything about hip-hop that has been good for this country. And it's not—before you get carried away—this has nothing to do with race. Because there are just as many hip-hopping white kids and Asian kids as there are hip-hopping black kids. It's a problem of a culture that values prison more than college; a culture that values rap and destruction of community values more than it does poetry; a culture that can't stand education. It's that culture that can't get control of itself." —MISSISSIPPI STATE SENATOR CHRIS MCDANIEL (R)

_____

_____

_____

"We believe that it is not our role to censor the creative expression of artists."
—PHILIPPE DAUMAN, PRESIDENT & CEO OF VIACOM INC.

_____

_____

_____

"I don't think that the hip-hop community is responsible for youth violence, but I think they haven't fully stepped up to the responsibilities to change the attitudes among youth.

"I think that the hip-hop community musicians have such sway over our young people. That's where so much of their information is received. There's enormous potential for a positive message to be transmitted. There are a whole series of messages that could be sent to our young people and these rap artists, and hip hop artists they're creative enough that they can communicate that message in a way that will appeal to young people, so we just have to tap that creativity." —BARACK OBAMA

_____

_____

_____

OPEN MIC: PUTTING THE QUESTION TO YOU!

*Please answer the question below making sure that you
use textual evidence to support whatever claims(s) you assert.*

In your opinion, is violence an appropriate solution for resolving conflict?

_____

_____

_____

_____

_____

_____

_____

_____

_____

_____

_____

_____

_____

_____

_____

_____

_____

_____

_____

_____

_____

_____

_____

_____

I not only wanted to showcase lyrical skills but also continue to drop knowledge on the hip-hop community. I'm looking to elevate through my music, and through my music I educate.

—TALIB KWELI

UNIT 3
DETERMINE THE POINT OF VIEW AND AUTHOR'S PURPOSE

Essential Question

Does money buy happiness?

Mark Twain	Informational Text: Charts Blending Literacy and Numbers
Lil' Kim	Dunn, Gilbert, and Wilson
Drake	Remixing World Views and Points of View: Spirituality and Money
Lauryn Hill	J. Cole and Gordon Gecko
Rakim	

Voices in the unit

Standards-Based Literacy Skills Targeted

Determining Point of View

Inform, Persuade, Entertain: Discovering the Author's Purpose

Offering Evidence-Based Opinions

Exploring Secondary Purposes

Close Reading, Line-by-Line Analysis

Analyzing Informational Text

Reading Charts and Graphs

Analyzing International Voices

Writing: Making Claims and Providing Evidence

CLASSIC INTERPRETATION GUIDE
Question: Does money buy happiness?

Consider the following text:

> *Huck Finn's wealth and the fact that he was now under the Widow Douglas's protection introduced him into society—no, dragged him into it, hurled him into it—and his sufferings were almost more than he could bear. The widow's servants kept him clean and neat, combed and brushed…. He had to eat with knife and fork; he had to use napkin, cup, and plate; he had to learn his book, he had to go to church; he had to talk so properly that speech was becoming insipid in his mouth; whithersoever he turned, the bars and shackles of civilization shut him in and bound him hand and foot.*
> —MARK TWAIN, THE ADVENTURES OF TOM SAWYER

1. What is Huck Finn's point of view about money's relationship to happiness?

- Huck Finn clearly does not believe money buys happiness.

2. What evidence from the text can you provide to support your assertion?

- The text says that the "sufferings were almost more than he could bear." The text says that Huck was forced to be "clean and neat" and he had to "eat with fork and knife" and so on. Huck was, as Twain puts it, "shackled by civilization."

3. Explain why you either agree or disagree with Huck Finn's point of view about whether having a lot of money buys happiness. (Make sure to address a specific detail in the text to support your reasoning.)

Answers will vary.

_____

_____

There are three primary purposes behind why an author writes a piece of text.

To Inform	To Persuade	To Entertain
Authors seek to impart information, data, or facts about a subject.	Authors seek to change or alter a person's point of view about a subject.	Authors seek to delight, enthrall, charm, beguile, enamor, or amuse.

In your opinion, what is Mark Twain's primary purpose behind writing this text?

- Mark Twain's primary purpose is to entertain the reader.

What evidence from the text can you provide to support your assertion?

- Mark Twain's use of humor and irony—by twisting it so that Huck's sudden riches become an unwanted burden—brings smiles to the face of a reader. There is much comedy in the text (such as Huck's not wanting to be clean, neat, combed, and brushed).

Bonus: Go deeper into your analysis!

Can you identify a second possible author's purpose inside the text? (Make sure to cite a specific detail from the selection to support your reasoning.)

- A second possible purpose inside the text could be to persuade the readers that they, as the old saying goes, better be careful what they wish for. Huck's poverty had many drawbacks, but at least it offered him freedom. Wealth, as the text clearly says, "dragged and hurled" Huck into civilization—a place he did not want to go.

CLASSIC STUDENT WORKSHEET
Question: Does money buy happiness?

Consider the following text:

> *Huck Finn's wealth and the fact that he was now under the Widow Douglas's protection introduced him into society—no, dragged him into it, hurled him into it—and his sufferings were almost more than he could bear. The widow's servants kept him clean and neat, combed and brushed.... He had to eat with knife and fork; he had to use napkin, cup, and plate; he had to learn his book, he had to go to church; he had to talk so properly that speech was becoming insipid in his mouth; whithersoever he turned, the bars and shackles of civilization shut him in and bound him hand and foot.*
> —MARK TWAIN, THE ADVENTURES OF TOM SAWYER

What is Huck Finn's point of view about money's relationship to happiness?

_____

What evidence from the text can you provide to support your assertion?

_____

_____

Explain why you either agree or disagree with Huck Finn's point of view about whether having a lot of money buys happiness. (Make sure to cite a specific detail from the text to support your reasoning.)

_____

_____

There are three primary purposes behind why an author writes a piece of text.

To Inform	To Persuade	To Entertain
Authors seek to impart information, data, or facts about a subject.	Authors seek to change or alter a person's point of view about a subject.	Authors seek to delight, enthrall, charm, beguile, enamor, or amuse.

In your opinion, what is Mark Twain's primary purpose behind writing this text?

_____

What evidence from the text can you provide to support your assertion?

_____

_____

Bonus: Go deeper into your analysis!

Can you identify a second possible author's purpose inside the text? (Make sure to cite a specific detail from the selection to support your reasoning.)

_____

_____

_____

HIP-HOP INTERPRETATION GUIDE
Question: Does money buy happiness?

Consider the following text:

from "Money, Power & Respect" by The Lox (featuring Lil' Kim and DMX)

It's the key to life
Money, power, and respect, whatchu' need in life
Money, power, and respect, you'll be eatin' right
Money, power, and respect, help you sleep at night
You'll see the light, it's the key to life
Money, power, and respect
Money, power, and respect
Money, power, and respect

What is Lil' Kim's point of view about money's relationship to happiness?

- Lil' Kim believes that having a lot of money directly corresponds with happiness.

What evidence from the text can you provide to support your assertion?

- Lil' Kim states that money (along with power and respect) are "Whatchu' need in life" and that it is the "key to life." She also cites how it contributes to "eatin' right" and how it will "help you sleep at night."

Explain why you either agree or disagree with Lil' Kim's point of view about whether having a lot of money buys happiness. (Make sure to cite a specific detail from the text to support your reasoning.)

Answers will vary; however, having money contributes to "eatin' right"
and some of the other basic human necessities. There's a wants vs. needs aspect to this.

_____

_____

There are three primary purposes behind why an author writes a piece of text.

To Inform	To Persuade	To Entertain
Authors seek to impart information, data, or facts about a subject.	Authors seek to change or alter a person's point of view about a subject.	Authors seek to delight, enthrall, charm, beguile, enamor, or amuse.

In your opinion, what is Lil' Kim's primary purpose behind writing this text?

- Lil' Kim's primary purpose is to inform the reader of her views on wealth.

What evidence from the text can you provide to support your assertion?

- Lil' Kim's use of straightforward statements such as "It's the key to life" and "what you need in life" speak to what money (and power and respect) bring to a person (i.e., a sense of well-being that allows a person to eat well and rest easily). Additionally, the repetition works as a rhetorical device to further emphasize Lil' Kim's point.

Bonus: Go deeper into your analysis!

Can you identify a second possible author's purpose inside the text? (Make sure to cite a specific detail from the selection to support your reasoning.)

- A second possible purpose is to entertain the reader. Because it's a rap song, there is a pleasing entertainment value to be found in both the phonetics and the phrasing of the text.

HIP-HOP STUDENT WORKSHEET
Question: Does money buy happiness?

Consider the following text:

from "Money, Power & Respect" by The Lox (featuring Lil' Kim and DMX)

It's the key to life
Money, power, and respect, whatchu' need in life
Money, power, and respect, you'll be eatin' right
Money, power, and respect, help you sleep at night
You'll see the light, it's the key to life
Money, power, and respect
Money, power, and respect
Money, power, and respect

What is Lil' Kim's point of view about money's relationship to happiness?

_____

What evidence from the text can you provide to support your assertion?

_____

_____

Explain why you either agree or disagree with Lil' Kim's point of view about whether having a lot of money buys happiness. (Make sure to cite a specific detail from the text to support your reasoning.)

_____

_____

There are three primary purposes behind why an author writes a piece of text.

To Inform	To Persuade	To Entertain
Authors seek to impart information, data, or facts about a subject.	Authors seek to change or alter a person's point of view about a subject.	Authors seek to delight, enthrall, charm, beguile, enamor, or amuse.

In your opinion, what is Lil' Kim's primary purpose behind writing this text?

_____

What evidence from the text can you provide to support your assertion?

_____

_____

_____

Bonus: Go deeper into your analysis!

Can you identify a second possible author's purpose inside the text? (Make sure to cite a specific detail from the selection to support your reasoning.)

_____

_____

INTERPRETATION GUIDE
Question: Does money buy happiness?

Consider the following text:

from "Dreams Money Can Buy" by Drake

I got car money, fresh start money
I want Saudi money, I want art money...
Dreams money can buy
They told me it's like a high, and it wasn't a lie

What is Drake's point of view about money's relationship to happiness?

- Drake believes there is a direct relationship between money and happiness (or at least, elation).

What evidence from the text can you provide to support your assertion?

- Drake makes the point that he's had the experience of having attained immense sums of wealth and that the mythology around having tons of money being a "high," as he says, "wasn't a lie."

Explain why you either agree or disagree with Drake's point of view about whether having a lot of money buys happiness. (Make sure to cite a specific detail from the text to support your reasoning.)

Answers will vary.

There are three primary purposes behind why an author writes a piece of text.

To Inform	To Persuade	To Entertain
Authors seek to impart information, data, or facts about a subject.	Authors seek to change or alter a person's point of view about a subject.	Authors seek to delight, enthrall, charm, beguile, enamor, or amuse.

In your opinion, what is Drake's primary purpose behind this text?

- Drake's primary purpose is to inform his listeners that once they have lots and lots of cash, money becomes like a drug (which can be both a good and bad thing).

What evidence from the text can you provide to support your assertion?

- Drake cleverly twists the word "high" in such a way that on one side, he makes the experiences of being fabulously wealthy feel exhilarating and enviable, but like all drugs, on the other side he infers that wealth has a dark side that can cause people to lose themselves and their inner value scheme to its seductive power.

Bonus: Go deeper into your analysis!

Can you identify a second possible purpose in the text? (Make sure to cite a specific detail from the selection to support your reasoning.)

- A second purpose is to entertain the audience. Because almost everyone wants to live the fantasy of being fabulously rich, Drake allows the audience to vicariously live through him when he says "and it wasn't a lie," a line that connotes he's taken a deep drink of the good life as an international celebrity.

STUDENT WORKSHEET
Question: Does money buy happiness?

Consider the following text:

from "Dreams Money Can Buy" by Drake

I got car money, fresh start money
I want Saudi money, I want art money…
Dreams money can buy
They told me it's like a high, and it wasn't a lie

What is Drake's point of view about money's relationship to happiness?

_____

What evidence from the text can you provide to support your assertion?

_____

_____

Explain why you either agree or disagree with Drake's point of view about whether having a lot of money buys happiness. (Make sure to cite a specific detail from the text to support your reasoning.)

_____

_____

There are three primary purposes behind why an author writes a piece of text.

To Inform	To Persuade	To Entertain
Authors seek to impart information, data, or facts about a subject.	Authors seek to change or alter a person's point of view about a subject.	Authors seek to delight, enthrall, charm, beguile, enamor, or amuse.

In your opinion, what is Drake's primary purpose behind this text?

_____

_____

What evidence from the text can you provide to support your assertion?

_____

_____

_____

Bonus: Go deeper into your analysis!

Can you identify a second possible purpose in the text? (Make sure to cite a specific detail from the selection to support your reasoning.)

_____

_____

_____

HIP-HOP INTERPRETATION GUIDE
Question: Does money buy happiness?

Consider the following text:

from "Final Hour" by Lauryn Hill

You can get the money
You can get the power
But keep your eyes on the Final Hour

I'm about to change the focus from the richest to the brokest
I wrote this opus, to reverse the hypnosis
Whoever's closest to the line's gonna win it
You gonna fall trying to ball while my team win the pennant

What is Lauryn Hill's point of view about money's relationship to happiness?

- Lauryn Hill believes that money will not buy true happiness.

What evidence from the text can you provide to support your assertion?

- Hill states people need to "keep your eyes on the Final Hour," asserting that no matter how much money people have, at the end of their days, it's the content of their character and the way they lived their lives that are most important—and this is the path to true happiness. The reference to "reverse the hypnosis" also supports Hill's belief that money doesn't buy happiness despite its false appearance of doing so.

Explain why you either agree or disagree with Lauren Hill's point of view about whether having a lot of money buys happiness. (Make sure to cite a specific detail from the text to support your reasoning.)

Answers will vary.

_____

_____

There are three primary purposes behind why an author writes a piece of text.

To Inform	To Persuade	To Entertain
Authors seek to impart information, data, or facts about a subject.	Authors seek to change or alter a person's point of view about a subject.	Authors seek to delight, enthrall, charm, beguile, enamor, or amuse.

In your opinion, what is Lauryn Hill's primary purpose behind writing this text?

- Lauryn Hill's primary purpose is to persuade readers that no amount of money can save them from facing their Final Hour (i.e., Judgment Day).

What evidence from the text can you provide to support your assertion?

- Hill encourages her audience to "change the focus" from the popular cultural narrative of strive to be rich at all costs to there are more important things than wealth and consumption. Furthermore, "the Final Hour" hovers like an omen above the text as the crux of her argument, compounded by the phrase "you gonna fall trying to ball."

Bonus: Go deeper into your analysis!

Can you identify a second possible author's purpose inside the text? (Make sure to cite a specific detail from the selection to support your reasoning.)

- A second possible purpose is to entertain the reader. Because it's a rap song, the entertainment value of the text is always part of the equation.

HIP-HOP STUDENT WORKSHEET
Question: Does money buy happiness?

Consider the following text:

from "Final Hour" by Lauryn Hill

You can get the money
You can get the power
But keep your eyes on the Final Hour

I'm about to change the focus from the richest to the brokest
I wrote this opus, to reverse the hypnosis
Whoever's closest to the line's gonna win it
You gonna fall trying to ball while my team win the pennant

What is Lauryn Hill's point of view about money's relationship to happiness?

_____

What evidence from the text can you provide to support your assertion?

_____

_____

Explain why you either agree or disagree with Lauren Hill's point of view about whether having a lot of money buys happiness. (Make sure to cite a specific detail from the text to support your reasoning.)

_____

_____

There are three primary purposes behind why an author writes a piece of text.

To Inform	To Persuade	To Entertain
Authors seek to impart information, data, or facts about a subject.	Authors seek to change or alter a person's point of view about a subject.	Authors seek to delight, enthrall, charm, beguile, enamor, or amuse.

In your opinion, what is Lauryn Hill's primary purpose behind writing this text?

_____

_____

What evidence from the text can you provide to support your assertion?

_____

_____

Bonus: Go deeper into your analysis!

Can you identify a second possible author's purpose inside the text? (Make sure to cite a specific detail from the selection to support your reasoning.)

_____

_____

CLOSE READING: COUPLET BY COUPLET INTERPRETATION GUIDE
Question: Does money buy happiness?

There are three primary purposes behind why an author writes a piece of text.

To Inform	To Persuade	To Entertain
Authors seek to impart information, data, or facts about a subject.	Authors seek to change or alter a person's point of view about a subject.	Authors seek to delight, enthrall, charm, beguile, enamor, or amuse.

Some authors masterfully weave all three purposes together in a single piece of text.

*Examine: **"Paid in Full" by Eric B and Rakim***

1. Thinking of a master plan
2. Cause ain't nothing but sweat inside my hand
3. So I dig into my pocket, all my money spent
4. So I dig deeper, but still coming up with lint
5. So I start my mission, leave my residence
6. Thinking how could I get some dead presidents

How does Rakim inform, persuade, and entertain inside the text of the first couplet?

1. Thinking of a master plan
2. Cause ain't nothing but sweat inside my hand

How does Rakim inform?	How does Rakim persuade?	How does Rakim entertain?
Rakim informs the audience that times are hard and he is flat broke. *Evidence:* He says, "Nothing but sweat inside my hand."	He persuades us he's a man of action who won't sit idly by despite society's perception of him. *Evidence:* He says, "Thinking of a master plan."	Rakim entertains the audience with a unique description of his poverty. *Evidence:* He says, "Ain't nothing but sweat inside my hand" (i.e., no money).

How does Rakim inform, persuade, and entertain inside the text of the second couplet?

3. So I dig into my pocket, all my money spent
4. So I dig deeper, but still coming up with lint

How does Rakim inform?	How does Rakim persuade?	How does Rakim entertain?
Rakim informs us that it's as bad as bad can get money-wise. He's totally without means. *Evidence:* "I dig deeper, but still come up with lint."	He persuades us he's both determined and desperate. *Evidence:* He digs into his pocket not once but twice (determined) but it's empty.	Rakim entertains the audience with a second unique description of his poverty. *Evidence:* He says, "I dig deeper, but still come up with lint."

How does Rakim inform, persuade, and entertain inside the text of the third couplet?

5. So I start my mission, leave my residence
6. Thinking how could I get some dead presidents

How does Rakim inform?	How does Rakim persuade?	How does Rakim entertain?
Rakim informs us that he's taking action in his quest to earn money ("dead presidents"). Evidence: "I start my mission."	He persuades us he's a man of character, bold and courageous. *Evidence:* "Leave my residence" infers a confident man willing to take risks (on a "mission).	He entertains with yet another rhyming couplet to cap off his text. *Evidence:* The aesthetic value of the AA-BB-CC rhyme scheme throughout.

CLOSE READING: COUPLET BY COUPLET STUDENT WORKSHEET
Question: Does money buy happiness?

There are three primary purposes behind why an author writes a piece of text.

To Inform	To Persuade	To Entertain
Authors seek to impart information, data, or facts about a subject.	Authors seek to change or alter a person's point of view about a subject.	Authors seek to delight, enthrall, charm, beguile, enamor, or amuse.

Some authors masterfully weave all three purposes together in a single piece of text.

Examine: "Paid in Full" by Eric B and Rakim

1. Thinking of a master plan
2. Cause ain't nothing but sweat inside my hand
3. So I dig into my pocket, all my money spent
4. So I dig deeper, but still coming up with lint
5. So I start my mission, leave my residence
6. Thinking how could I get some dead presidents

How does Rakim inform, persuade, and entertain inside the text of the first couplet?

1. Thinking of a master plan
2. Cause ain't nothing but sweat inside my hand

How does Rakim inform?	How does Rakim persuade?	How does Rakim entertain?
_____	_____	_____
_____	_____	_____
Evidence: _____	*Evidence:* _____	*Evidence:* _____

How does Rakim inform, persuade, and entertain inside the text of the second couplet?

3. So I dig into my pocket, all my money spent
4. So I dig deeper, but still coming up with lint

How does Rakim inform?	How does Rakim persuade?	How does Rakim entertain?
_____	_____	_____
_____	_____	_____
Evidence: _____	*Evidence:* _____	*Evidence:* _____

How does Rakim inform, persuade, and entertain inside the text of the third couplet?

5. So I start my mission, leave my residence
6. Thinking how could I get some dead presidents

How does Rakim inform?	How does Rakim persuade?	How does Rakim entertain?
_____	_____	_____
_____	_____	_____
Evidence: _____	*Evidence:* _____	*Evidence:* _____

BLENDING LITERACY AND NUMBERS: WORKING WITH INFORMATIONAL TEXT
Question: Does money buy happiness?

When 1,000 people were asked which recording studio they would rather be employed at for the next 3 years...

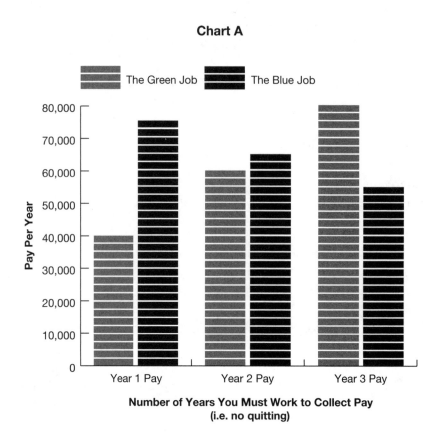

Chart A

The results surprised researchers (even though the work was the same).

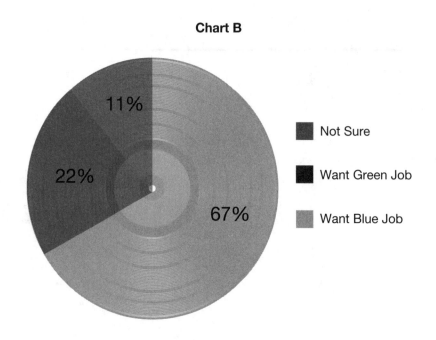

Chart B

**BLENDING LITERACY AND NUMBERS:
WORKING WITH INFORMATIONAL TEXT INTERPRETATION GUIDE**

Question: Does money buy happiness?

Based on the information provided in Chart A and Chart B, provide a short response:

1. Consider the point of view of the researchers. Why do you think they might have found the results surprising?
(Be sure to cite a piece of evidence from the chart to support your assertion.)

The researchers probably found the results surprising because if you total up the salary for three years' worth of work at each job, the green pays $15,000 more than the blue does and most people, they presumed, would have wanted more money.

2. Consider the point of view of the blue group. Why do you believe they chose the blue job over the green job?
(Be sure to cite a piece of evidence from the chart to support your assertion.)

The blue group offered a salary increase each year. Their pay after Year 1 goes from $40K to $60K, and then the pay after Year 2 goes from $60K to $80K. Getting a raise each year most probably influenced their decision.

3. Consider the point of view of the green group. Why do you believe they chose the green job over the blue job?
(Be sure to cite a piece of evidence from the chart to support your assertion.)

Even though the salary dropped from year to year, the green group offered more total pay for three years' worth of work ($180,000 compared to $195,000).

4. Consider the point of view of the "not sure" group. Why do you believe they were undecided?
(Be sure to cite a piece of evidence from the chart to support your assertion.)

When it came to choosing between earning significant annual raises (as Chart A shows via the bar graph with a salary increase) or taking a pay cut each year while earning more total money (as Chart A shows when the totals are added), the "not sure" group—as Chart B demonstrates in the yellow section of the pie chart—simply could not decide which job would bring them more happiness/satisfaction.

5. What does the chart demonstrate about the relationship between money and happiness?
(Be sure to cite a piece of evidence to support your assertion.)

The chart demonstrates that a majority of people in this survey believe that a sense of career salary growth translates to more happiness and fulfillment than a decreasing annual salary does and even if the total pay is greater, the personal unhappiness that comes with a salary decrease is not worth the trade-off.

6. If you were offered both the green and the blue jobs, which would you take and why?
(Be sure to cite evidence from the chart to explain your choice.)

Answers will vary.

_____

_____

_____

_____

_____

BLENDING LITERACY AND NUMBERS:
WORKING WITH INFORMATIONAL TEXT STUDENT WORKSHEET
Question: Does money buy happiness?

Based on the information provided in Chart A and Chart B, provide a short response:

1. Consider the point of view of the researchers. Why do you think they might have found the results surprising? (Be sure to cite a piece of evidence from the chart to support your assertion.)

_____

_____

_____

2. Consider the point of view of the blue group. Why do you believe they chose the blue job over the green job? (Be sure to cite a piece of evidence from the chart to support your assertion.)

_____

_____

_____

3. Consider the point of view of the green group. Why do you believe they chose the green job over the blue job? (Be sure to cite a piece of evidence from the chart to support your assertion.)

_____

_____

_____

4. Consider the point of view of the "not sure" group. Why do you believe they were undecided? (Be sure to cite a piece of evidence from the chart to support your assertion.)

_____

_____

_____

_____

5. What does the chart demonstrate about the relationship between money and happiness? (Be sure to cite a piece of evidence to support your assertion.)

_____

_____

_____

_____

6. If you were offered both the green and the blue jobs, which would you take and why? (Be sure to cite evidence from the chart to explain your choice.)

_____

_____

_____

_____

INFORMATIONAL TEXT INTERPRETATION GUIDE
Question: Does money buy happiness?

Consider the text:

> *Why doesn't a whole lot more money make us a whole lot more happy? One answer is that the things that bring happiness simply aren't for sale. This sentiment is lovely, popular, and almost certainly wrong. Money allows people to live longer and healthier lives, to buffer themselves against worry and harm, to have leisure time to spend with friends and family, and to control the nature of their daily activities—all of which are sources of happiness. Wealthy people don't just have better toys; they have better nutrition and better medical care, more free time, and more meaningful labor—more of just about every ingredient in the recipe for a happy life. And yet, they aren't that much happier than those who have less. If money can buy happiness, then why doesn't it?*
> —ELIZABETH DUNN, DANIEL GILBERT, AND TIMOTHY WILSON,
> JOURNAL OF CONSUMER PSYCHOLOGY, VOL. 21, ISSUE 2, APRIL 2011

What is the authors' point of view about money's relationship to happiness?

- The authors' point of view is that money should—but does not—buy happiness.

What evidence from the text can you provide to support your assertion?

- The authors cite specific things money does buy (better health, more leisure time, etc.) and that these things do deliver happiness, but they point out that people who have more money "aren't that much happier than people who have less."

Explain why you either agree or disagree with the authors' point of view about whether having a lot of money buys happiness. (Make sure to cite a specific detail from the text to support your reasoning.)

Answers will vary.

_____

_____

There are three primary purposes behind why an author writes a piece of text.

To Inform	To Persuade	To Entertain
Authors seek to impart information, data, or facts about a subject.	Authors seek to change or alter a person's point of view about a subject.	Authors seek to delight, enthrall, charm, beguile, enamor, or amuse.

In your opinion, what is the authors' primary purpose behind writing this text?

- The authors' primary purpose is to inform readers that money will not buy happiness.

What evidence from the text can you provide to support your assertion?

- They state that people with money have "just about every ingredient in the recipe for a happy life. And yet, they aren't that much happier than those who have less."

Bonus: Go deeper into your analysis!

Can you identify a second possible authors' purpose inside the text? (Make sure to cite a specific detail from the selection to support your reasoning.)

- Another purpose might be that the authors are seeking to persuade readers against buying into the popular belief that money will buy happiness. By stating that money could and even should buy happiness (i.e., "Wealthy people don't just have better toys; they have better nutrition and better medical care") while stating that it does not, the authors are challenging readers to rethink a widely held societal misperception.

INFORMATIONAL TEXT STUDENT WORKSHEET
Question: Does money buy happiness?

Consider the text:

Why doesn't a whole lot more money make us a whole lot more happy? One answer is that the things that bring happiness simply aren't for sale. This sentiment is lovely, popular, and almost certainly wrong. Money allows people to live longer and healthier lives, to buffer themselves against worry and harm, to have leisure time to spend with friends and family, and to control the nature of their daily activities—all of which are sources of happiness. Wealthy people don't just have better toys; they have better nutrition and better medical care, more free time, and more meaningful labor—more of just about every ingredient in the recipe for a happy life. And yet, they aren't that much happier than those who have less. If money can buy happiness, then why doesn't it?
—ELIZABETH DUNN, DANIEL GILBERT, AND TIMOTHY WILSON,
JOURNAL OF CONSUMER PSYCHOLOGY, VOL. 21, ISSUE 2, APRIL 2011

What is the authors' point of view about money's relationship to happiness?

_____

What evidence from the text can you provide to support your assertion?

_____

_____

Explain why you either agree or disagree with the authors' point of view about whether having a lot of money buys happiness. (Make sure to cite a specific detail from the text to support your reasoning.)

_____

_____

There are three primary purposes behind why an author writes a piece of text.

To Inform	To Persuade	To Entertain
Authors seek to impart information, data, or facts about a subject.	Authors seek to change or alter a person's point of view about a subject.	Authors seek to delight, enthrall, charm, beguile, enamor, or amuse.

In your opinion, what is the authors' primary purpose behind writing this text?

_____

What evidence from the text can you provide to support your assertion?

_____

_____

Bonus: Go deeper into your analysis!

Can you identify a second possible authors' purpose inside the text? (Make sure to cite a specific detail from the selection to support your reasoning.)

_____

_____

_____

REMIXING WORLD VIEWS AND POINTS OF VIEW: SPIRITUALITY AND MONEY INTERPRETATION GUIDE
Question: Does money buy happiness?

Determine whether Lauryn Hill would agree or disagree with the following statements. Why or why not? Use evidence from either text to support your answer.

1. "Blessed are you who are poor, for yours is the kingdom of God. Blessed are you who are hungry now, for you will be filled. Blessed are you who weep now, for you will laugh." —JESUS FROM LUKE 6:20-21

- Lauryn Hill would most likely agree with this statement because she also speaks of changing the "focus" to the poor (i.e., the "brokest"). Furthermore, "the Final Hour" can allude to what is beyond this worldly life, which could to some be "the kingdom of God."

2. "It is easier for a camel to go through the eye of a needle than for a rich man to enter the kingdom of God." —MATTHEW 19:23-26

- Lauryn Hill would most likely agree with this statement because we can infer that her "team" that wins "the pennant" could be poised for some sort of greater glory (i.e., "the kingdom of God").

Determine whether Huck Finn would agree or disagree with the following statements. Why or why not? If possible, use specific evidence from either text to support your answer.

1. "The wealth which enslaves the owner isn't wealth." —YORUBA PROVERB

- Huck Finn would agree with this Yoruba proverb because he experienced the "shackles of civilization" that "bound him hand and foot," that came with his newfound wealth.

2. "If the rich could hire the poor to die for them, the poor would make a very nice living." —JEWISH PROVERB

- Huck Finn would agree with this Jewish proverb because he was "dragged" and "hurled" into a society with "servants," rules, and protocols.

Determine whether Lil' Kim would agree or disagree with the following statements. Why or why not? If possible, use specific evidence from either text to support your answer.

1. "But woe to you who are rich, for you have received your consolation. Woe to you who are full now, for you will be hungry. Woe to you who are laughing now, for you will mourn and weep." —JESUS FROM LUKE 6:24-25

- Lil' Kim would most likely disagree with Jesus's statement because she believes that "money" is a key to life and that she is "laughing now" because of her financial status.

2. "Money is sharper than the sword." —ASHANTI PROVERB

- Lil' Kim would most likely agree with this proverb. She uses repetition to emphasize the connections between money, power, and respect, and therefore, she believes money can be viewed as powerful (i.e., "sharper than the sword").

REMIXING WORLD VIEWS AND POINTS OF VIEW: SPIRITUALITY AND MONEY INTERPRETATION GUIDE

Question: Does money buy happiness?

Determine whether Drake would agree or disagree with the following statements. Why or why not? If possible, use specific evidence from either text to support your answer.

1. *"Competition in worldly increase diverts you."* —QURAN 102:1

- Drake would disagree with this verse from the Quran because he seems to believe that competitiveness has fueled his achievement (in a positive manner).

2. *"Poverty is my pride."* —THE PROPHET MOHAMMED

- Drake might agree with Mohammed because he knows money makes you "high" and his words connote that getting high can be a double-edged sword with a downside. Poverty, however, brings humility and no such exposure to ego-driven power plays.

Determine whether Rakim would agree or disagree with the following statements. Why or why not? If possible, use specific evidence from either text to support your answer.

1. *"Each individual is responsible for his misfortunes, his fate. It is wrong to expect help to fall from above, as a gift: Wealth has to be deserved. Work is one of the commandments of Our Lord the Creator!"* —EMPEROR HAILE SELASSIE, RASTAFARIAN

- We can infer from "Paid in Full" that Rakim mostly likely does agree with Emperor Selassie because he is "thinking of a master plan" and therefore taking individual responsibility for his situation.

2. *"Money is like water, try to grab it and it flows away, open your hands and it will move towards you."* —BUDDHA

- It is hard to say; however, Rakim has "nothing but sweat inside his hand" and "lint" in his pocket, so most likely he would disagree with the Buddha.

Determine whether Dunn, Gilbert, and Wilson would agree or disagree with the following statements. Why or why not? If possible, use specific evidence from either text to support your answer.

1. *If your happiness depends on money, you will never be happy with yourself. Be content with what you have; rejoice in the way things are. When you realize there is nothing lacking, the whole world belongs to you.* —LAO-TZU, TAO TE CHING

- Dunn, Gilbert, and Wilson would agree with Lao-tzu because they assert that "the things that bring happiness are not for sale."

2. *"He who loves money will not be satisfied with money."* —THE TALMUD

- Dunn, Gilbert, and Wilson would agree with this statement for reasons stated in the previous question, and furthermore implies that money can't satisfy fully against "worry and harm."

REMIXING WORLD VIEWS AND POINTS OF VIEW: RELIGION, SPIRITUALITY, AND MONEY STUDENT WORKSHEET
Question: Does money buy happiness?

Determine whether Lauryn Hill would agree or disagree with the following statements. Why or why not? Use evidence from either text to support your answer.

1. "Blessed are you who are poor, for yours is the kingdom of God. Blessed are you who are hungry now, for you will be filled. Blessed are you who weep now, for you will laugh." —JESUS FROM LUKE 6:20-21

_____

_____

2. "It is easier for a camel to go through the eye of a needle than for a rich man to enter the kingdom of God." —MATTHEW 19:23-26

_____

_____

Determine whether Huck Finn would agree or disagree with the following statements. Why or why not? If possible, use specific evidence from either text to support your answer.

1. "If the rich could hire the poor to die for them, the poor would make a very nice living." —JEWISH PROVERB

_____

_____

2. "The wealth which enslaves the owner isn't wealth." —YORUBA PROVERB

_____

_____

Determine whether Lil' Kim would agree or disagree with the following statements. Why or why not? If possible, use specific evidence from either text to support your answer.

1. "But woe to you who are rich, for you have received your consolation. Woe to you who are full now, for you will be hungry. Woe to you who are laughing now, for you will mourn and weep." —JESUS FROM LUKE 6:24-25

_____

_____

2. "Money is sharper than the sword." —ASHANTI PROVERB

_____

_____

REMIXING WORLD VIEWS AND POINTS OF VIEW: RELIGION, SPIRITUALITY, AND MONEY STUDENT WORKSHEET

Question: Does money buy happiness?

Determine whether Drake would agree or disagree with the following statements. Why or why not? If possible, use specific evidence from either text to support your answer.

1. "Competition in worldly increase diverts you." —QURAN 102:1

_____

_____

2. "Poverty is my pride." —THE PROPHET MOHAMMED

_____

_____

Determine whether Rakim would agree or disagree with the following statements. Why or why not? If possible, use specific evidence from either text to support your answer.

1. "Each individual is responsible for his misfortunes, his fate. It is wrong to expect help to fall from above, as a gift: Wealth has to be deserved. Work is one of the commandments of Our Lord the Creator!" —EMPEROR HAILE SELASSIE, RASTAFARIAN

_____

_____

2. "Money is like water, try to grab it and it flows away, open your hands and it will move towards you." —BUDDHA

_____

_____

Determine whether Dunn, Gilbert, and Wilson would agree or disagree with the following statements. Why or why not? If possible, use specific evidence from either text to support your answer.

1. If your happiness depends on money, you will never be happy with yourself. Be content with what you have; rejoice in the way things are. When you realize there is nothing lacking, the whole world belongs to you. —LAO-TZU, TAO TE CHING

_____

_____

2. "He who loves money will not be satisfied with money." —THE TALMUD

_____

_____

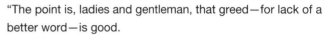

DETERMINE THE POINT OF VIEW: MORE VOICES INTERPRETATION GUIDE
Does money buy happiness?

Consider the following two texts…

For what's money without happiness?

Or hard times without the people you love

Though I'm not sure what's 'bout to happen next

I asked for strength from the Lord up above

—J. COLE, LOVE YOURZ

"The point is, ladies and gentleman, that greed—for lack of a better word—is good.

Greed is right.

Greed works.

Greed clarifies, cuts through, and captures the essence of the evolutionary spirit.

Greed, in all of its forms—greed for life, for money, for love, for knowledge—has marked the upward surge of mankind."

—GORDON GECKO, FROM THE MOVIE WALL STREET, WRITTEN BY OLIVER STONE

What is J. Cole's point of view about money's relationship to happiness? Be sure to provide textual evidence to support your assertion.

- J. Cole clearly believes that having financial means without having inner fulfillment is empty and emotionally hollow. His first line, a question which rhetorically asks, "What's money without happiness?" supports this assertion.

What is Gordon Gecko's point of view about money's relationship to happiness? Be sure to provide textual evidence to support your assertion.

- The character from the movie Wall Street clearly believes that money—tons and tons of it—is the fuse that ignites all other positive experiences. The rapacious pursuit of money is a good thing. Gordon Gecko's statement that "Greed in all its forms … has marked the upward surge of mankind" supports this assertion.

Speculate what J. Cole would say to Gordon Gecko about money's relationship to happiness. Make sure to include a piece of textual evidence to support your claim.

- J. Cole would probably tell Gordon Gecko that his ideas are misguided and that his values are skewed. Strength, as J. Cole says in the text, comes from the "Lord up above" and not from an immense number of worldly possessions.

Speculate what Gordon Gecko would say to J. Cole about money's relationship to happiness. Make sure to include a piece of textual evidence to support your claim.

- Gordon Gecko would probably tell J. Cole that his ideas are naive and out of touch with the way the real world works. A deep hunger for money is good, according to Gecko, as evidenced by the argumentative lines he offers in greed's defense: "Greed is right. Greed works. Greed clarifies, cuts through, and captures the essence of the evolutionary spirit."

A famous, ancient proverb says, "You aren't wealthy until you have something that money can't buy."
Please cite 3 things you have that money can't buy.

1. Answers will vary._____

2. Answers will vary._____

3. Answers will vary._____

DETERMINE THE POINT OF VIEW: MORE VOICES STUDENT WORKSHEET
Does money buy happiness?

Consider the following two texts…

For what's money without happiness?

Or hard times without the people you love

Though I'm not sure what's 'bout to happen next

I asked for strength from the Lord up above

—J. COLE, LOVE YOURZ

"The point is, ladies and gentleman, that greed—for lack of a better word—is good.

Greed is right.

Greed works.

Greed clarifies, cuts through, and captures the essence of the evolutionary spirit.

Greed, in all of its forms—greed for life, for money, for love, for knowledge—has marked the upward surge of mankind."

—GORDON GECKO, FROM THE MOVIE WALL STREET, WRITTEN BY OLIVER STONE

What is J. Cole's point of view about money's relationship to happiness?
Be sure to provide textual evidence to support your assertion.

_____

_____

_____

What is Gordon Gecko's point of view about money's relationship to happiness?
Be sure to provide textual evidence to support your assertion.

_____

_____

_____

Speculate what J. Cole would say to Gordon Gecko about money's relationship to happiness.

_____

_____

_____

Speculate what Gordon Gecko would say to J. Cole about money's relationship to happiness.

_____

_____

_____

A famous, ancient proverb says, "You aren't wealthy until you have something that money can't buy."
Please cite 3 things you have that money can't buy.

1. _____

2. _____

3. _____

OPEN MIC: PUTTING THE QUESTION TO YOU!

*Please answer the question below making sure that you
use textual evidence to support whatever claims(s) you assert.*

In your opinion, is violence an appropriate solution for resolving conflict?

_____
_____
_____
_____
_____
_____
_____
_____
_____
_____
_____
_____
_____
_____
_____
_____
_____
_____
_____
_____
_____
_____
_____
_____
_____
_____

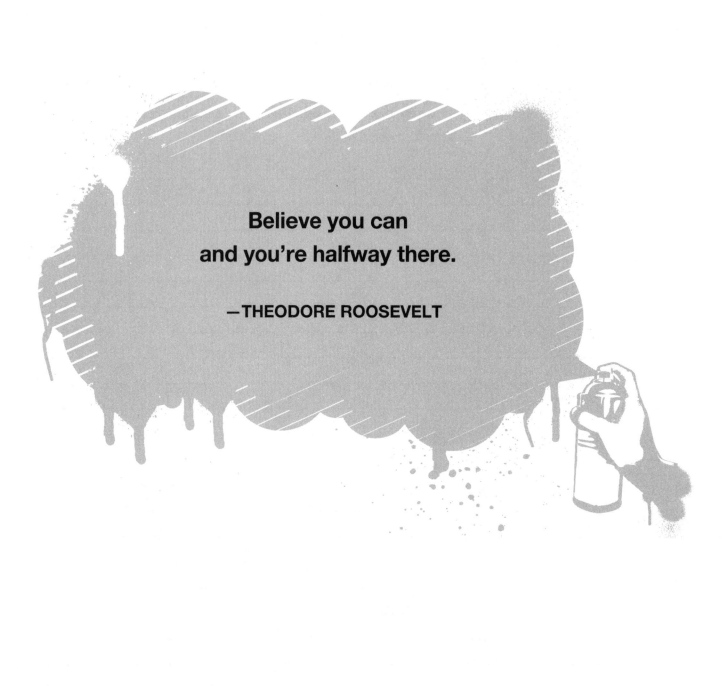

Believe you can
and you're halfway there.

—THEODORE ROOSEVELT

UNIT 4
ASCERTAIN THE CENTRAL IDEA AND SYNTHESIZE TEXTS

Essential Question

Is it more advantageous to be a boy or a girl?

Voices in the unit

Byron Hurt	Gender in Schools Bar Graph
Hilary Thayer Hamann	Informational Text: The Glass Ceiling
Salt-N-Pepa	XXL Magazine
The U.S. Census	Nicki Minaj
bell hooks	Charli Baltimore
William Draves	Lil' Kim

Standards-Based Literacy Skills Targeted

Ascertain the Central Idea

Synthesize Texts

Cite Details

Support Assertions with Textual Evidence

Explain Your Reasoning

Demonstrate Reading Comprehension

Analyze Themes

Scrutinize Informational Text

Read Charts and Graphs

Writing: Making Claims and Providing Evidence

INTERPRETATION GUIDE
Is it more advantageous to be a boy or a girl?

Consider the following two texts…

Text 1

"Every black man that goes in the [hip-hop recording] studio has always got two people in his head: him, in terms of who he really is, and the thug that he feels he has to project."

—BYRON HURT, FROM THE DOCUMENTARY FILM HIP-HOP: BEYOND BEATS & RHYMES

Text 2

"Boys will be boys, that's what people say. No one ever mentions how girls have to be something other than themselves altogether. We are to stifle the same feelings that boys are encouraged to display. We are to use gossip as a means of policing ourselves."

—HILARY THAYER HAMANN, FROM HER NOVEL ANTHROPOLOGY OF AN AMERICAN GIRL

What central idea do the two texts share?

- The two texts share the idea that people need to suppress or hide their true inner selves because their gender requires them to put on a front/wear a mask.

Cite one specific detail from Text 1 that provides evidence for your assertion.

- The speaker points out that black men in hip-hop recording studios feel they must "project a thug image" even if that is not who they really are.

Cite one specific detail from Text 2 that provides evidence for your assertion.

- The speaker points out that girls have "to stifle the same feelings that boys are encouraged to display" and "be something other than themselves altogether."

Which of the following sentiments would BOTH authors from the texts above be most likely to agree with and why? (Explain your reasoning with evidence from the texts.)

NOTE: There is more than one possible correct answer.

A. Keepin' it real means I don't hide the real me for anyone.

B. No matter who you are on this planet, you gotta wear a mask to navigate your way through society.

C. Men don't ever have to hide their true feelings like women do.

D. Being me means being a person who experiences inner conflict.

E. I don't really care what anyone else thinks.

F. No matter who you are, it always feels like the other gender always has it easier.

G. Girls are meaner to one another than boys are to one another.

My Answer Choice: *Answer can be B or D or F*

My Reasoning:

- Answer B makes sense because both texts speak to the idea of covering up your true inner self.
- Answer D makes sense because both texts speak to the idea that presenting a false front to the outer world causes inner turmoil for the authentic self that lives within.
- Answer F makes sense because both texts imply that the opposite gender doesn't have to go through the "masquerades" that their own sex must to navigate their world/culture/community.

STUDENT WORKSHEET
Is it more advantageous to be a boy or a girl?

Consider the following two texts:

Text 1	Text 2
"Every black man that goes in the [hip-hop recording] studio has always got two people in his head: him, in terms of who he really is, and the thug that he feels he has to project." —BYRON HURT, FROM THE DOCUMENTARY FILM BEYOND BEATS & RHYMES	"Boys will be boys, that's what people say. No one ever mentions how girls have to be something other than themselves altogether. We are to stifle the same feelings that boys are encouraged to display. We are to use gossip as a means of policing ourselves." —HILARY THAYER HAMANN, FROM HER NOVEL ANTHROPOLOGY OF AN AMERICAN GIRL

What central idea do the two texts share?

_____

Cite one specific detail from Text 1 that provides evidence for your assertion.

_____

Cite one specific detail from Text 2 that provides evidence for your assertion.

_____

Which of the following sentiments would BOTH authors from the texts above be most likely to agree with and why? (Explain your reasoning with evidence from the texts.)

_____

NOTE: *There is more than one possible correct answer.*

A. Keepin' it real means I don't hide the real me for anyone.

B. No matter who you are on this planet, you gotta wear a mask to navigate your way through society.

C. Men don't ever have to hide their true feelings like women do.

D. Being me means being a person who experiences inner conflict.

E. I don't really care what anyone else thinks.

F. No matter who you are, it always feels like the other gender always has it easier.

G. Girls are meaner to one another than boys are to one another.

My Answer Choice: _____

My Reasoning:

_____

_____

_____

_____

_____

ASCERTAIN THE CENTRAL IDEA AND SYNTHESIZE TEXTS
Is it more advantageous to be a boy or a girl?

Consider the following three texts…

Text 1: Informational Text

According to the U.S. Census Bureau's report on income and poverty (2013), women make nearly $11,000 less each year than men. That translates to a woman making 78 cents for every one dollar made by a man for doing the exact same work.

Text 2: Hip-Hop

The thing that makes me mad and crazy, upset

Got to break my neck just to get my respect

Go to work and get paid less than a man

When I'm doin' the same dang thing that he can

—SALT-N-PEPA, FROM "AINT NOTHIN BUT A SHE THING"

Text 3: Bar Graph

Individual median income by gender and educational attainment in the year 2013

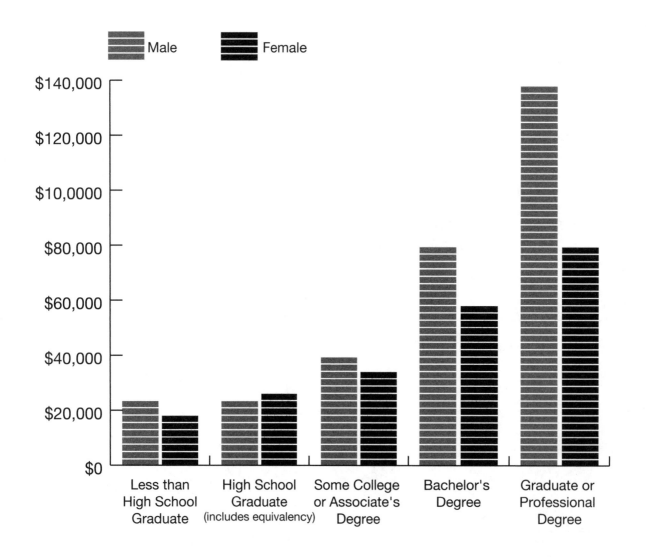

INTERPRETATION GUIDE
Is it more advantageous to be a boy or a girl?

Based on the information provided, please answer the following questions:

What central idea do all three texts share?

- All three of the texts support the idea that women are not compensated in a manner that is equal to men for doing the same work.

Cite one specific detail from Text 1 that provides evidence for your assertion.

- The U.S. Census Bureau provides hard data, which states that woman "make nearly $11,000 less each year than men" and that that difference "translates to a woman making 78 cents for every one dollar made by a man for doing the exact same work."

Cite one specific detail from Text 2 that provides evidence for your assertion.

- Salt-N-Pepa clearly make the case that they do not feel the manner in which women are compensated is fair when they say "Got to break my neck just to get my respect" as well as when they point out "Go to work and get paid less than a man."

Cite one specific detail from Text 3 that provides evidence for your assertion.

- The bar graph shows a consistency of data across every level of the chart whereby men make more (in terms of income) than women do regardless of their level of educational attainment for the same work.

Which of the following sentiments would ALL authors from the texts be most likely to agree with and why? (Explain your reasoning with evidence from the texts.)

NOTE: There is more than one possible correct answer.

A. Men clearly outperform women in the workforce and therefore deserve higher compensation.

B. Women have good reason to complain.

C. All American men think it's fair that women get paid less for equal work.

D. Some women make more than men do for doing the same job.

E. Employers in the United States show clear gender bias.

F. What matters most is the quality of your work.

G. Salary differences between men and women are a significant issue.

My Answer Choice: *Answer can be B or E or G*

My Reasoning:

- Answer B makes sense because all three of the texts show that woman are being unfairly compensated—and where there is unfairness, there is just reason to complain.
- Answer E makes sense because all three of the texts emphasize the idea that there is rampant discrimination based solely on the sex of the worker.
- Answer G makes sense because it can be reasonably inferred that one of the purposes behind all three of the texts is to illuminate a major societal inequality that requires remediation.

STUDENT WORKSHEET
Is it more advantageous to be a boy or a girl?

Based on the information provided, please answer the following questions:

What central idea do all three texts share?

_____

_____

Cite one specific detail from Text 1 that provides evidence for your assertion.

_____

_____

_____

Cite one specific detail from Text 2 that provides evidence for your assertion.

_____

_____

_____

Cite one specific detail from Text 3 that provides evidence for your assertion.

_____

_____

_____

Which of the following sentiments would ALL authors from the texts be most likely to agree with and why? (Explain your reasoning with evidence from the text.)

NOTE: There is more than one possible correct answer.

A. Men clearly outperform women in the workforce and therefore deserve higher compensation.

B. Women have good reason to complain.

C. All American men think it's fair that women get paid less for equal work.

D. Some women make more than men do for doing the same job.

E. Employers in the United States show clear gender bias.

F. What matters most is the quality of your work.

G. Salary differences between men and women are a significant issue.

My Answer Choice: _____

My Reasoning:

_____

_____

_____

_____

_____

ASCERTAIN THE CENTRAL IDEA AND SYNTHESIZE TEXTS
Is it more advantageous to be a boy or a girl?

Consider the following three texts…

Text 1

"Males today live in a world that pays them the most attention when they are violently acting out."

—BELL HOOKS, FROM HER BOOK
WE REAL COOL

Text 2

"The very same behaviors for which boys are punished in school are behaviors which boys are rewarded for when they enter the workforce. This is because taking risks, being entrepreneurial, being individualistic are all behaviors that lead to success in today's workforce but today's schools, in contrast, were meant to prepare youth for factory jobs and the office where conformity, teamwork, and 'being normal and docile' are valued. It's ironic that what is bad behavior for boys in school is good behavior for young men in the workplace."

—ADAPTED FROM THE WORK OF WILLIAM A. DRAVES, PRESIDENT OF THE LEARNING RESOURCES NETWORK (LERN)

Text 3: Bar Graph

Gender comparison in schools

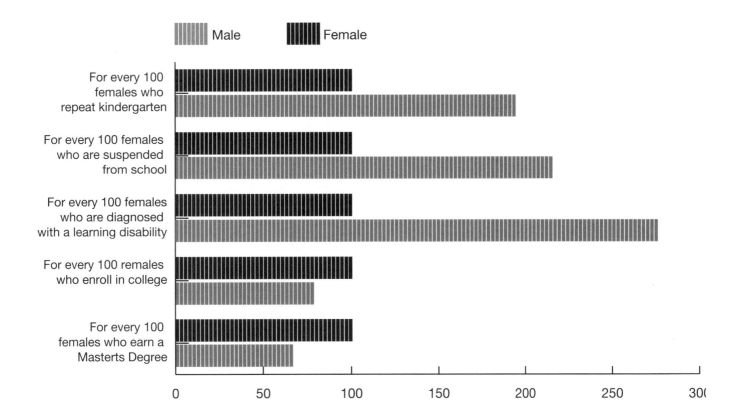

INTERPRETATION GUIDE
Is it more advantageous to be a boy or a girl?

Based on the information provided, please answer the following questions:

What central idea do all three texts share?

- All three of the texts support the idea that society is not only treating boys differently than girls but in a more "negative and disadvantageous" manner as well.

Cite one specific detail from Text 1 that provides evidence for your assertion.

- When hooks states boys are being positively rewarded for behavior that is so clearly negative, it supports the idea that boys are fighting an uphill battle, particularly as compared to girls (who are not rewarded for violent behavior by the world).

Cite one specific detail from Text 2 that provides evidence for your assertion.

- Drave clearly states that boys are being sent conflicting messages when he cites the irony about how school is punishing boys for behaving in ways that the workplace (once they leave school) will ultimately reward them for (while inferring that girls are not being sent conflicting messages of the same sort).

Cite one specific detail from Text 3 that provides evidence for your assertion.

- The bar graph shows a lot of data that is clearly skewed against boys (as compared to girls) including their rate of retention in kindergarten, their rate of suspension from school, their overdiagnosis of learning disabilities, and so on.

Which of the following sentiments would ALL authors from the texts be most likely to agree with and why? (Explain your reasoning with evidence from the text.)

NOTE: There is more than one possible correct answer.

A. Boys and girls are clearly being treated as equals in a way that is admirable.

B. Girls have good reason to believe they are being shortchanged by society.

C. Society needs to rethink the manner in which today's boys are being raised.

D. Gender differences affect the manner in which children are treated, both in school and in society at large.

E. Teachers, parents, and workforce employers do not have any cause for concern about the well-being of today's young men.

F. The expectations society holds for boys and the expectations society holds for girls are quite different.

G. When all is said and done, it's still much easier to be a boy than it is to be a girl.

My Answer Choice: *Answer can be C or D or F*

My Reasoning:

- Answer C makes sense because all three of the texts show that boys are being raised by society in ways that appear to be potentially detrimental.
- Answer D makes sense because all three of the texts suggest—if not emphasize—the idea that boys are being treated differently than girls are being treated.
- Answer F makes sense because all three texts imply that girls are being held to a different set of standards than boys are.

STUDENT WORKSHEET
Is it more advantageous to be a boy or a girl?

Based on the information provided, please answer the following questions:

What central idea do all three texts share?

_____

_____

Cite one specific detail from Text 1 that provides evidence for your assertion.

_____

_____

Cite one specific detail from Text 2 that provides evidence for your assertion.

_____

_____

Cite one specific detail from Text 3 that provides evidence for your assertion.

_____

_____

Which of the following sentiments would ALL authors from the texts be most likely to agree with and why?
(Explain your reasoning with evidence from the text.)

NOTE: There is more than one possible correct answer.

A. Boys and girls are clearly being treated as equals in a way that is admirable.

B. Girls have good reason to believe they are being shortchanged by society.

C. Society needs to rethink the manner in which today's boys are being raised.

D. Gender differences affect the manner in which children are treated, both in school and in society at large.

E. Teachers, parents, and workforce employers do not have any cause for concern about the well-being of today's young men.

F. The expectations society holds for boys and the expectations society holds for girls are quite different.

G. When all is said and done, it's still much easier to be a boy than it is to be a girl.

My Answer Choice: _____

My Reasoning:

_____

_____

_____

_____

THE GLASS CEILING

A ceiling made of glass would be transparent. See-through. A barely detectable barrier. The phrase "glass ceiling" refers to a invisible yet very real barriers in the workforce—particularly as they apply to women. Theoretically, women ought to be able to rise to the same heights as men in their professional aspirations.

In reality, obstacles exist.

Studies show these barriers have nothing to do with anything other than gender. The job one does ought to be the most critical factor in deciding who gets best rewarded for their efforts. Often, however, as many women know, this is not the case.

The invisible barriers that often hold women back from achieving the same level of power, status, and achievement as men have been given a name: the "glass ceiling." It's a term that describes whatever elements keep women from attaining power and success equal to men's.

When women make exceptional gains in the workforce, they are often said to "break through the glass ceiling."

According to surveys of professional women:

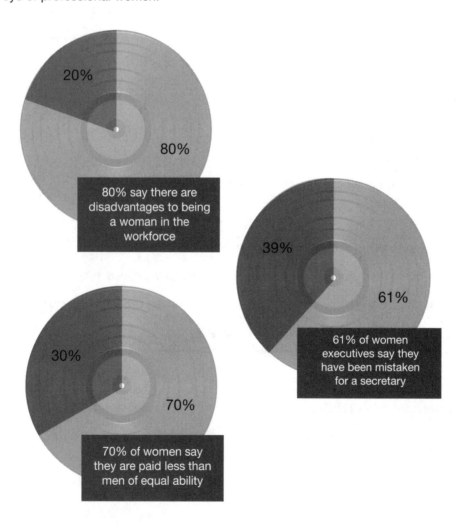

20%

80%

80% say there are disadvantages to being a woman in the workforce

39%

61%

61% of women executives say they have been mistaken for a secretary

30%

70%

70% of women say they are paid less than men of equal ability

One of the biggest challenges for women to break through the glass ceiling is that all too often the obstructions women face are not overt. Hindrances are not in plain sight. They are subtle and underground and hard to put a finger on.

Much has changed over the past 50 years in the United States. Yet for women at work, there is still much more change that needs to occur.

INTERPRETATION GUIDE
Is it more advantageous to be a boy or a girl?

What is the central idea of the text?

- The central idea of the text is that there is a phenomenon known as the "glass ceiling," which speaks to a barrier that prohibits many women from earning the same amount of power, status, or pay in the U.S. workforce as men do.

Cite one specific detail from the text that provides evidence for your assertion.

- One piece of evidence from the text is when the author asserts: "Theoretically, women ought to be able to rise to the same heights as men in their professional aspirations." But then the author goes on to state: "In reality, obstacles exist." This proves there is inequality.

Cite another specific detail from the text that provides evidence for your assertion.

- A second piece of evidence from the text is when the author talks about how when women do attain equality, they are said to "break through the glass ceiling." This proves that the barriers are not insurmountable but also that they are not fabrications.

Cite one specific detail from one of the charts embedded in the text that provides evidence for your assertion.

- Answers will vary, but all three of the charts point to how a majority of women surveyed believe that the phenomenon of discrimination against women in the workforce is a very real occurrence in their professional lives.

Which of the following sentiments would the author of the text be most likely to agree with and why? (Explain your reasoning with evidence from the text.)

NOTE: There is more than one possible correct answer.

A. Even high-ranking female executives face gender-based bias at their jobs.

B. In low-level jobs, gender really doesn't matter that much because the pay is minimal.

C. Men try to be biased on purpose because they feel women are inferior.

D. Women don't mind that there is a glass ceiling in the workforce.

E. The glass ceiling highlights unfair business practices.

F. Women are complaining about things that can't be changed.

G. In the U.S. quest for equal rights for women, the battle is not over yet.

My Answer Choice: *Answer can be A or E or G*

My Reasoning:

- Answer A makes sense because the text points to how even "executive level women" feel as if gender bias exists (or is a hurdle they have encountered).
- Answer E makes sense because one of the main focal points of the entire text is about how business practices are unfair because discrimination based solely on gender differences exists in the U.S. workforce.
- Answer G makes sense because the battle for equal rights can't end until all gender-based bias is eradicated from the workforce.

STUDENT WORKSHEET
Is it more advantageous to be a boy or a girl?

What is the central idea of the text?

_____

_____

Cite one specific detail from the text that provides evidence for your assertion.

_____

_____

_____

Cite another specific detail from the text that provides evidence for your assertion.

_____

_____

_____

Cite one specific detail from one of the charts embedded in the text that provides evidence for your assertion.

_____

_____

Which of the following sentiments would the author of the text be most likely to agree with and why? (Explain your reasoning with evidence from the text.)

NOTE: There is more than one possible correct answer.

A. Even high-ranking female executives face gender-based bias at their jobs.

B. In low-level jobs, gender really doesn't matter that much because the pay is minimal.

C. Men try to be biased on purpose because they feel women are inferior.

D. Women don't mind that there is a glass ceiling in the workforce.

E. The glass ceiling highlights unfair business practices.

F. Women are complaining about things that can't be changed.

G. In the U.S. quest for equal rights for women, the battle is not over yet.

My Answer Choice: _____

My Reasoning:

_____

_____

_____

_____

DOES A GLASS CEILING EXIST IN HIP-HOP? INTERPRETATION GUIDE

"Since its beginnings, hip-hop has been a Boys Club, with female MCs often ignored or pushed to the side, boxed into the background or assuming the 'eye candy' role in music videos." —XXL MAGAZINE	"I do not see myself as a female rapper anymore, I'm sorry. I see myself as a rapper. I've worked with the greats and I've held my own with the greats and they respect me. So I should respect myself enough to see myself the same way they see themselves." -NICKI MINAJ
It's a male-dominated industry. You have to be an MC and a businessman so people will respect you. —CHARLI BALTIMORE	"I think females make really great music and they need to be acknowledged. We don't get the acknowledgment that men get. Sometimes we don't get the acknowledgment that men get and we sell more records. Sometimes we don't get the same push as male artists." —LIL' KIM

What central idea unifies all the quotes?

▪ Women in the world of hip-hop do not receive the same treatment as their male counterparts in the world of hip-hop do.

Cite one specific detail from one of the pieces of text that provides evidence for your assertion.

▪ Though all four quotes speak to the main idea, Charli Baltimore clearly provides evidence for the above assertion when she says, "It's a male-dominated industry."

Cite a second specific detail from a different piece of text that provides evidence for your assertion.

▪ Yet again, all four quotes speak to the main idea but XXL provides clear evidence for the above assertion when the magazine states, "female MCs [have been] often ignored or pushed to the side, boxed into the background or assuming the 'eye candy' role in music videos."

Which of the following sentiments would ALL of the quoted authors of the texts be most likely to agree with and why? (Explain your reasoning with evidence.)

A. The business of hip-hop does not care whether you are male or female.

B. Audiences and industry professionals respect female rappers and treat them as equal to their male counterparts.

C. The women of hip-hop aren't as talented as the men in hip-hop, so therefore the women don't deserve the same acclaim as the men do.

D. A bias against female artists exists in hip-hop.

My Answer Choice: *Answer is D*

My Reasoning:

All four quotes reflect the sentiment that an unfair bias exists against women in hip-hop. Only answer D addresses this

DOES A GLASS CEILING EXIST IN HIP-HOP? STUDENT WORKSHEET

Consider the following four texts...

"Since its beginnings, hip-hop has been a Boys Club, with female MCs often ignored or pushed to the side, boxed into the background or assuming the 'eye candy' role in music videos."

—XXL MAGAZINE

"I do not see myself as a female rapper anymore, I'm sorry. I see myself as a rapper. I've worked with the greats and I've held my own with the greats and they respect me. So I should respect myself enough to see myself the same way they see themselves."

-NICKI MINAJ

It's a male-dominated industry. You have to be an MC and a businessman so people will respect you.

—CHARLI BALTIMORE

"I think females make really great music and they need to be acknowledged. We don't get the acknowledgment that men get. Sometimes we don't get the acknowledgment that men get and we sell more records. Sometimes we don't get the same push as male artists."

—LIL' KIM

What central idea unifies all the quotes?

_____

_____

Cite one specific detail from the one of the pieces of text that provides evidence for your assertion.

_____

_____

Cite a second specific detail from a different piece of text that provides evidence for your assertion.

_____

_____

Which of the following sentiments would ALL of the quoted authors of the texts be most likely to agree with and why? (Explain your reasoning with evidence.)

A. The business of hip-hop does not care whether you are male or female.

B. Audiences and industry professionals respect female rappers and treat them as equal to their male counterparts.

C. The women of hip-hop aren't as talented as the men in hip-hop, so therefore the women don't deserve the same acclaim as the men do.

D. A bias against female artists exists in hip-hop.

My Answer Choice: _____

My Reasoning:

_____

_____

_____

OPEN MIC: PUTTING THE QUESTION TO YOU!

*Please answer the question below making sure that you
use textual evidence to support whatever claims(s) you assert.*

In your opinion, is violence an appropriate solution for resolving conflict?

_____

_____

_____

_____

_____

_____

_____

_____

_____

_____

_____

_____

_____

_____

_____

_____

_____

_____

_____

_____

_____

_____

_____

_____

_____

_____

Your work is going to fill a large part of your life, and the only way to be truly satisfied is to do what you believe is great work. And the only way to do great work is to love what you do. If you haven't found it yet, keep looking. Don't settle. As with all matters of the heart, you'll know when you find it.

—STEVE JOBS

UNIT 5
LANGUAGE AND CONTEXT: ASSESSING STYLE, MEANING, AUDIENCE, AND WORD CHOICE

Essential Question

How does language give people power?

Voices in the unit

Sonia Sotomayor
Big L
Todd Boyd
Mos Def
Henry Hazlitt

Tall Paul
Steven Pressfield
Rachel Stokes and James Garner
Ice Cube

Standards-Based Literacy Skills Targeted:

Understanding Author's Purpose
Deducing Tone and Mood
Determining Proper Protocol
Exploring Digital Considerations
Comprehending Style
Providing Evidence-Based Reasoning
Reading Closely
Examining Word Choice
Writing Across Modalities
Unearthing Meaning
Strong vs. Weak Arguments
Writing: Making Claims and Providing Evidence

INTERPRETATION GUIDE
Question: How does language give people power?

At a minimum, we are all **trilingual** (i.e., we express ourselves in at least three languages), varying the manner in which we communicate according to our audience and purpose.

1. Please cite three instances when it is most appropriate to express yourself using STANDARD, FORMAL, TRADITIONAL ENGLISH and explain why.

Instance #1: In a school/academic setting, reason why standard English is appropriate: When your audience is teachers, your purpose becomes expressing yourself in a manner that educators find acceptable and appropriate. Thus, you would use standard English.

Instance #2: In a conventional business atmosphere, reason why standard English is appropriate: When your audience is businesspeople, your purpose becomes expressing yourself in a manner that people in the conventional business world find acceptable and appropriate (i.e. standard English.) And business can be lost by violating this protocol.

Instance #3: In a speaking with people in a position of authority environment, reason why standard English is appropriate: When your audience is people in a position of authority (i.e., hotel managers, courtroom judges, etc.), your purpose becomes expressing yourself in a manner that people in positions of authority find acceptable and appropriate. Thus, you would use standard English. (And not doing so might lead to negative consequences.)

2. Please cite three instances when it is most appropriate to express yourself using LUNCHTIME, STREET, NONFORMAL ENGLISH and explain why.

Instance #1: When hanging out with friends, reason why lunchtime English is appropriate:

When your audience is your friends, your purpose becomes expressing yourself in a manner that your peers find acceptable and appropriate. Thus, you would use lunchtime English.

Instance #2: Playing sports or games, reason why lunchtime English is appropriate: When your audience is people with whom you are playing sports or games, your purpose becomes expressing yourself in a manner that the other players find acceptable and appropriate. Thus, you would use lunchtime English.

Instance #3: At social gatherings, reason why lunchtime English is appropriate: When your audience is people who are getting together with the intention to simply have fun, your purpose becomes expressing yourself in a manner that is relaxed, acceptable, and appropriate. Thus, you would use lunchtime English.

3. Please cite three instances when it is most appropriate to express yourself using TEXT MESSAGE, DIGITAL, SOCIAL MEDIA ENGLISH and explain why.

Instance #1: When sending a text , reason why text message English is appropriate: When your audience is people who will be reading your texts, your purpose becomes expressing yourself in a manner appropriate to the medium. Thus, you would use text message English.

Instance #2: When communicating in the world of social media, reason why text message English is appropriate: When your audience is people with whom you will be interacting digitally in the world of social media, your purpose becomes expressing yourself in a manner appropriate to the medium. Thus, you would use text message English.

Instance #3: In a handwritten, informal note, reason why text message English is appropriate: Text message English can extend to the world of handwritten notes (e.g., "I luv u!" written on a Post-it). When your audience is informal, your purpose becomes expressing yourself in a manner that is both appropriate to the medium and intimate. Thus, text message English is sometimes the correct choice.

STUDENT WORKSHEET

Question: How does language give people power?

At a minimum, we are all **trilingual** (i.e., we express ourselves in at least three languages), varying the manner in which we communicate according to our audience and purpose.

1. Please cite three instances when it is most appropriate to express yourself using STANDARD, FORMAL, TRADITIONAL ENGLISH and explain why.

Instance #1: _____

Reason why standard English is appropriate: _____

_____

Instance #2: _____

Reason why standard English is appropriate: _____

_____

Instance #3: _____

Reason why standard English is appropriate: _____

_____

2. Please cite three instances when it is most appropriate to express yourself using LUNCHTIME, STREET, NONFORMAL ENGLISH and explain why.

Instance #1: _____

Reason why lunchtime English is appropriate: _____

_____

Instance #2: _____

Reason why lunchtime English is appropriate: _____

_____

Instance #3: _____

Reason why lunchtime English is appropriate: _____

_____

3. Please cite three instances when it is most appropriate to express yourself using TEXT MESSAGE, DIGITAL, SOCIAL MEDIA ENGLISH and explain why.

Instance #1: _____

Reason why text message English is appropriate: _____

_____

Instance #2: _____

Reason why text message English is appropriate: _____

_____

Instance #3: _____

Reason why text message English is appropriate: _____

_____

INTERPRETATION GUIDE
Question: How does language give people power?

"When everyone at school is speaking one language, and a lot of your classmates' parents also speak it, and you go home and see that your community is different, there is a sense of shame attached to that. It really takes growing up to treasure the specialness of being different."
—SONIA SOTOMAYOR, FIRST LATINA U.S. SUPREME COURT JUSTICE

1. How would you categorize the style of expression on display in the text above?
- The style is formal, standard English.

2. Cite a piece of evidence from the text that supports your claim.
- The proper use of the apostrophe s in the line "your classmates' parents" demonstrates excellent grammar (grammar being a staple of formal English).

3. Explain the author's purpose behind choosing this style of expression for her words (i.e., Who is Sotomayor's intended audience?).
- Sotomayor chooses to communicate in standard formal English because her audience is obviously sophisticated enough to understand the reflective nature of her comment—and the protocol for mature audiences is typically formal English.

4. Cite a piece of evidence from the text that supports your assertion.
- When Sotomayor speaks about the "sense of shame," there is an adultlike wisdom on display, proving that she is speaking in a grown-up to grown-up type manner.

5. Sotomayor says, "It really takes growing up to treasure the specialness of being different." In your own words, explain what she means by this.
- Sotomayor means that as a child she felt that being different was something to feel embarrassed about but after becoming an adult she realizes that being different is something to be cherished.

Tone is the author's attitude toward the subject.	**Mood** is the effect an author's words have on an audience (i.e., how the words make us feel).
What is Sotomayor's tone in the text above?	What mood has Sotomayor created in the audience in the text above?
Sotomayor's tone is thoughtful, reflective, philosophical.	*The mood created by Sotomayor's words is one of respect and admiration.*
Cite a specific word or phrase from the text that supports your assertion and explain how it does so.	Cite a specific word or phrase from the text that supports your assertion and explain how it does so.
The phrase "It really takes growing up to treasure the specialness of being different" demonstrates the insight one gleans from looking backwards at events from the past.	*The mentioning of the word "shame" conveys a sentiment that when Sotomayor was a little girl she felt bad but as an adult she's overcome her insecurities—and most of us admire people who overcome inner obstacles in a positive way.*

STUDENT WORKSHEET

Question: How does language give people power?

"When everyone at school is speaking one language, and a lot of your classmates' parents also speak it, and you go home and see that your community is different, there is a sense of shame attached to that. It really takes growing up to treasure the specialness of being different."
—SONIA SOTOMAYOR, FIRST LATINA U.S. SUPREME COURT JUSTICE

1. How would you categorize the style of expression on display in the text above?

   _____

2. Cite a piece of evidence from the text that supports your claim.

   _____

   _____

3. Explain the author's purpose behind choosing this style of expression for her words
   (i.e., Who is Sotomayor's intended audience?).

   _____

   _____

4. Cite a piece of evidence from the text that supports your assertion.

   _____

   _____

5. Sotomayor says, "It really takes growing up to treasure the specialness of being different." In your own words, explain what she means by this.

   _____

   _____

Tone is the author's attitude toward the subject.	**Mood** is the effect an author's words have on an audience (i.e., how the words make us feel).
What is Sotomayor's tone in the text above?	What mood has Sotomayor created in the audience in the text above?
_____	_____
_____	_____
_____	_____
Cite a specific word or phrase from the text that supports your assertion and explain how it does so.	Cite a specific word or phrase from the text that supports your assertion and explain how it does so.
_____	_____
_____	_____
_____	_____

INTERPRETATION GUIDE

Question: How does language give people power?

From the song "Ebonics" by Big L

Jealous is jelly, your food box is your belly
To guerrilla mean to use physical force
You took an L, you took a loss
To show off mean floss
I know you like the way I'm freaking it
I talk with slang and I'ma never stop speaking it

1. How would you categorize the style of expression on display in the text above?
- The style of expression is informal, lunchtime English (slang).

2. Cite a piece of evidence from the text that supports your claim.
- Many examples exist such as "like the way I'm freaking it" or the fact that Big L even directly says, "I talk with slang."

3. Explain the author's purpose behind choosing this style of expression for his words (i.e., Who is Big L's intended audience?).
- Big L chooses to express himself with slang because his intended audience is fans of hip-hop (and informal, lunchtime English is their protocol for expression).

4. Cite a piece of evidence from the text that supports your assertion.
- When Big L asserts that "I'ma never stop speaking it," he is standing up for all the like-minded members of the hip-hop community.

5. Big L says, "I talk with slang and I'ma never stop speaking it." In your own words, explain what he means by this.
- Big L's words are defiant and in your face and the meaning is clear: he—and all hip-hoppas—talk in a stylized manner that can't be suppressed or stopped (even though they know it rubs the establishment the wrong way).

Tone is the author's attitude toward the subject.	**Mood** is the effect an author's words have on an audience (i.e., how the words make us feel).
What is Big L's tone in the text above?	What mood has Big L created in the audience in the text above?
Big L's tone is rebellious and bold and cocky.	*For fans of hip-hop, Big L's words most likely create a mood of admiration (and head nods of "Heck, yeah"). For detractors of hip-hop, the sentiment is probably the opposite.*
Cite a specific word or phrase from the text that supports your assertion and explain how it does so.	Cite a specific word or phrase from the text that supports your assertion and explain how it does so.
Each time Big L defines his slang for a layperson serves as an example of this (i.e., *"Jealous is jelly, your food box is your belly / To guerrilla mean to use physical force / You took an L, you took a loss"* and so on)	*When Big L says, "I know you like the way I'm freaking it," he's giving a double message: for those who do like the way he's freaking it, they agree, and for those who do not like the way he is freaking it, he is implying that they can go take a hike because he and his kind don't care.*

STUDENT WORKSHEET
Question: How does language give people power?

From the song "Ebonics" by Big L

Jealous is jelly, your food box is your belly
To guerrilla mean to use physical force
You took an L, you took a loss
To show off mean floss
I know you like the way I'm freaking it
I talk with slang and I'ma never stop speaking it

1. How would you categorize the style of expression on display in the text above?

_____

2. Cite a piece of evidence from the text that supports your claim.

_____

_____

3. Explain the author's purpose behind choosing this style of expression for his words
(i.e., Who is Big L's intended audience?).

_____

_____

4. Cite a piece of evidence from the text that supports your assertion.

_____

_____

5. Big L says, "I talk with slang and I'ma never stop speaking it." In your own words, explain what he means by this.

_____

_____

Tone is the author's attitude toward the subject.	**Mood** is the effect an author's words have on an audience (i.e., how the words make us feel).
What is Big L's tone in the text above?	What mood has Big L created in the audience in the text above?
_____	_____
_____	_____
Cite a specific word or phrase from the text that supports your assertion and explain how it does so.	Cite a specific word or phrase from the text that supports your assertion and explain how it does so.
_____	_____
_____	_____
_____	_____

INTERPRETATION GUIDE
Question: How does language give people power?

"Hip-hop is inherently political, the language is political. It uses language as a weapon—not a weapon to violate or not a weapon to offend, but a weapon that pushes the envelope, that provokes people, makes people think." —TODD BOYD

1. How would you categorize the style of expression on display in the text above?
- The style of expression is formal, standard English.

2. Cite a piece of evidence from the text that supports your claim.
- Boyd's use of proper grammar (i.e., from the dash to the commas) as well as his purposeful avoidance of slang (i.e., no street words) buttresses this claim.

3. Explain the author's purpose behind choosing this style of expression for his words (i.e., Who is Boyd's intended audience?).
- Boyd's purpose for using formal, standard English is because he wants to address his intended audience on their own terms in their own language. In other words, he is aiming his ideas at people who might not be convinced that the language of hip-hop has merit. People who readily accept the value of hip-hop culture are not his primary aim; people who might be dubious about hip-hop's credibility are in his sights.

4. Cite a piece of evidence from the text that supports your assertion.
- In the very first line, Boyd explains that "hip-hop is inherently political." People well versed in hip-hop already know this. People unfamiliar with the merits of hip-hop are typically from the traditional (and conservative) cultural establishment, where the language is formal and quite proper.

5. Boyd says, "it [hip-hop] uses language as a weapon." In your own words, explain what he means by this.
- When Boyd says that "hip-hop uses language as a weapon," he is making the point that hip-hop is about more than just music; it's a cultural voice seeking to comment on social issues and even be a catalyst to create change in the community (as are all political voices).

Tone is the author's attitude toward the subject.

Mood is the effect an author's words have on an audience (i.e., how the words make us feel).

What is Boyd's tone in the text above?

Boyd's tone is authoritative and commanding, dignified and assertive.

Cite a specific word or phrase from the text that supports your assertion and explain how it does so.

Boyd's use of the phrase "hip-hop is inherently political" is a declarative statement. There's power, there's assurance, there's no real open door, as he continues his train of thought, for debating the point.

What mood has Boyd created in the audience in the text above?

Boyd creates a mood that is apt to polarize. He almost challenges the audience to take a stand, either agree and nod your head or disagree and shake your head. There's little middle ground.

Cite a specific word or phrase from the text that supports your assertion and explain how it does so.

When Boyd declares "hip-hop is a weapon that pushes the envelope" the in-your-face nature of the phrasing almost forces/ challenges an audience to choose sides, to agree or disagree.

STUDENT WORKSHEET

Question: How does language give people power?

"Hip-hop is inherently political, the language is political. It uses language as a weapon—not a weapon to violate or not a weapon to offend, but a weapon that pushes the envelope, that provokes people, makes people think." —TODD BOYD

1. How would you categorize the style of expression on display in the text above?

_____

2. Cite a piece of evidence from the text that supports your claim.

_____

_____

3. Explain the author's purpose behind choosing this style of expression for his words
(i.e., Who is Boyd's intended audience?).

_____

_____

_____

4. Cite a piece of evidence from the text that supports your assertion.

_____

_____

5. Boyd says, "it [hip-hop] uses language as a weapon." In your own words, explain what he means by this.

_____

_____

Tone is the author's attitude toward the subject.	**Mood** is the effect an author's words have on an audience (i.e., how the words make us feel).
What is Boyd's tone in the text above?	What mood has Boyd created in the audience in the text above?
_____	_____
_____	_____
_____	_____
Cite a specific word or phrase from the text that supports your assertion and explain how it does so.	Cite a specific word or phrase from the text that supports your assertion and explain how it does so.
_____	_____
_____	_____
_____	_____

INTERPRETATION GUIDE

Question: How does language give people power?

Embrace the bass with my dark ink fingertips
Used to speak the King's English
But caught a rash on my lips
So now my chat just like dis   —MOS DEF, FROM THE SONG "HIP-HOP"

1. How would you categorize the style of expression on display in the text above?
- The style of expression is informal, lunchtime English (slang).

2. Cite a piece of evidence from the text that supports your claim.
- The use of the phrase "so now my chat just like dis" is clearly slang.

3. Explain the author's purpose behind choosing this style of expression for his words (i.e., Who is Mos Def's intended audience?).
- Mos Def uses slang in order to be consciously defiant of the establishment's traditional rules. The author's purpose is to make a point about how he—as well as all members of his community of hip-hoppas—own the power to choose their own language and their means of expression. This text is a bold declaration of we do not need your permission to be who we are or who we want to be.

4. Cite a piece of evidence from the text that supports your assertion.
- Saying he "used to speak the King's English" is a recognition he was once indoctrinated by society into playing by its culturally acceptable rules. However, by forgoing the "King's English" (i.e., the words "used to" are in the past tense), Mos Def demonstrates his own free will to turn away from oppressive rules. The act is defiance personified.

5. Mos Def says he "caught a rash on my lips." In your own words, explain what he means by this.
- A rash is something most people would consider negative and unwanted, but Mos Def cleverly flips this idea on its head (through sarcasm) and conveys the notion that he (and his people) are happy to have this thing the establishment considers a rash. In other words, what power brokers consider sickness, he considers health.

Tone is the author's attitude toward the subject.

Mood is the effect an author's words have on an audience (i.e., how the words make us feel).

What is Mos Def's tone in the text above?

Mos Def's tone is independent and unconcerned with how his words will be received.

Cite a specific word or phrase from the text that supports your assertion and explain how it does so.

When Mos Def says "so now my chat just like dis," his purposeful use of [defiant] slang illustrates the point that he and his community are going to do what they are going to do whether the audience—or anyone else—likes it or approves of it.

What mood has Mos Def created in the audience in the text above?

Mos Def's words reflect an independence of spirit that can create a mood of admiration for those who agree with his sentiments or a mood of aggravation for those who disagree with his rebelliousness.

Cite a specific word or phrase from the text that supports your assertion and explain how it does so.

"My chat is just like dis" is obvious support, but also there's the phrase "with my dark ink fingertips," which implies he has spent a long time in solitude as a writer thinking about these ideas (i.e., dark ink from many hours of pen in hand) and it's not just off the cuff.

STUDENT WORKSHEET

Question: How does language give people power?

Embrace the bass with my dark ink fingertips
Used to speak the King's English
But caught a rash on my lips
So now my chat just like dis   —MOS DEF, FROM THE SONG "HIP-HOP"

1. How would you categorize the style of expression on display in the text above?

_____

2. Cite a piece of evidence from the text that supports your claim.

_____

_____

3. Explain the author's purpose behind choosing this style of expression for his words
(i.e., Who is Mos Def's intended audience?).

_____

_____

_____

4. Cite a piece of evidence from the text that supports your assertion.

_____

_____

5. Mos Def says he "caught a rash on my lips." In your own words, explain what he means by this.

_____

_____

Tone is the author's attitude toward the subject.	**Mood** is the effect an author's words have on an audience (i.e., how the words make us feel).
What is Mos Def's tone in the text above?	What mood has Mos Def created in the audience in the text above?
_____	_____
_____	_____
_____	_____
Cite a specific word or phrase from the text that supports your assertion and explain how it does so.	Cite a specific word or phrase from the text that supports your assertion and explain how it does so.
_____	_____
_____	_____
_____	_____

INTERPRETATION GUIDE
Question: How does language give people power?

"A man with a scant vocabulary will almost certainly be a weak thinker. The richer and more copious one's vocabulary and the greater one's awareness of fine distinctions and subtle nuances of meaning, the more fertile and precise is likely to be one's thinking. Knowledge of things and knowledge of the words for them grow together. If you do not know the words, you can hardly know the thing."
—HENRY HAZLITT, THINKING AS A SCIENCE

1. How would you categorize the style of expression on display in the text above?
- The style of expression is formal, standard English.

2. Cite a piece of evidence from the text that supports your claim.
- The keen, articulate precision of the first sentence illuminates the formality of Hazlitt (i.e., "A man with a scant vocabulary will almost certainly be a weak thinker").

3. Explain the author's purpose behind choosing this style of expression for his words (i.e., Who is Hazlitt's intended audience?).
- Hazlitt uses a very formal tone because it matches the sentiment he is trying to express. He is speaking to folks who have or appreciate intellectual acumen, and he is speaking to them in their own language, with strong potent words and ideas that are not tempered by slang or pandering.

4. Cite a piece of evidence from the text that supports your assertion.
- Hazlitt's sentence "The richer and more copious one's vocabulary and the greater one's awareness of fine distinctions and subtle nuances of meaning, the more fertile and precise is likely to be one's thinking" serves as a strong piece of evidence because it relates a complex idea expressed through rich words and a sophisticated structure.

5. Hazlitt says, "Knowledge of things and knowledge of the words for them grow together." In your own words, explain what he means by this.
- Hazlitt means that the wider your knowledge base grows, the more your vocabulary expands because the two—rich vocabularies and expansive intellects—are symbiotic (i.e., they interdependently grow together).

Tone is the author's attitude toward the subject.	**Mood** is the effect an author's words have on an audience (i.e., how the words make us feel).
What is Hazlitt's tone in the text above?	What mood has Hazlitt created in the audience in the text above?
Hazlitt's tone is formal yet admiring; he's not condescending about the presentation of his beliefs. It's matter of fact.	*Hazlitt creates a mood in his audience of appreciation (for his sentiments) as well as a bit of trepidation (because he's obviously a man of great intellect and many readers probably feel unsure about keeping up with his brain power).*
Cite a specific word or phrase from the text that supports your assertion and explain how it does so.	Cite a specific word or phrase from the text that supports your assertion and explain how it does so.
When Hazlitt says "If you do not know the words, you can hardly know the thing," he is almost scientific about his notion (i.e., he says it as if that is just simply the way the world operates).	*Hazlitt uses a lot of excellently well-chosen words such as "scant" or "copious," words that are both precious and "blue ribbon" in many ways. It's clear that as a thinker, he walks the talk.*

STUDENT GUIDE

Question: How does language give people power?

"A man with a scant vocabulary will almost certainly be a weak thinker. The richer and more copious one's vocabulary and the greater one's awareness of fine distinctions and subtle nuances of meaning, the more fertile and precise is likely to be one's thinking. Knowledge of things and knowledge of the words for them grow together. If you do not know the words, you can hardly know the thing."
—HENRY HAZLITT, THINKING AS A SCIENCE

1. How would you categorize the style of expression on display in the text above?

_____

2. Cite a piece of evidence from the text that supports your claim.

_____

_____

3. Explain the author's purpose behind choosing this style of expression for his words
(i.e., Who is Hazlitt's intended audience?).

_____

_____

4. Cite a piece of evidence from the text that supports your assertion.

_____

_____

5. Hazlitt says, "Knowledge of things and knowledge of the words for them grow together." In your own words, explain what he means by this.

_____

_____

Tone is the author's attitude toward the subject.	**Mood** is the effect an author's words have on an audience (i.e., how the words make us feel).
What is Hazlitt's tone in the text above?	What mood has Hazlitt created in the audience in the text above?
_____	_____
_____	_____
_____	_____
Cite a specific word or phrase from the text that supports your assertion and explain how it does so.	Cite a specific word or phrase from the text that supports your assertion and explain how it does so.
_____	_____
_____	_____
_____	_____

INTERPRETATION GUIDE
Question: How does language give people power?

From the song **"Prayers in a Song" by Tall Paul**

Inner-city Native raised by bright lights, skyscrapers
Born with dim prospects, little peace in living
As a child, hot-headed 'bout the fact I wasn't wild
Like they called my ancestors, imagined what it'd be
To live nomadic off the land and free
Instead I was full of heat like a furnace 'cuz I wasn't furnished
With language and traditional ways of my peeps

1. How would you categorize the style of expression on display in the text above?
- The style of expression is informal, lunchtime English (slang).

2. Cite a piece of evidence from the text that supports your claim.
- Although the lyric isn't slang heavy, it does reflect a hip-hop (informal aesthetic), and it also reflects on how his people were called "wild" and that he wasn't "furnished with language and traditional ways of my peeps." Overall these lines refer to how "other" ways of being and speaking are devalued, and therefore his language can be interpreted as undervalued.

3. Explain the author's purpose behind choosing this style of expression for his words (i.e., Who is Tall Paul's intended audience?).
- Tall Paul chooses to express himself with an autobiographical snapshot of his experience as an inner-city Native American, who has endured despite the challenges his people face, and his intended audience is a hip-hop community or Native American community of people who can access his lines.

4. Cite a piece of evidence from the text that supports your assertion.
- When Tall Paul asserts that "the fact I wasn't wild/Like they called my ancestors," he is standing up for his Native American community while highlighting the injustices against them; furthermore, he elaborates on this marginalization of his people and their language when he attests "I wasn't furnished with language and traditional ways of my peeps."

5. Tall Paul says, "Like my ancestors, imagined what it'd be/To live nomadic off the land and free." In your own words, explain what he means by this.
- Tall Paul is referring to the history of his ancestors, Native Americans (First Nation People), who once lived nomadic lives off of the land and were free to live according to their traditions and govern themselves.

Tone is the author's attitude toward the subject.	**Mood** is the effect an author's words have on an audience (i.e., how the words make us feel).
What is Tall Paul's tone in the text above?	What mood has Tall Paul's lyric created in the audience in the text above?
Tall Paul's tone is agitated and he feels slighted.	*The author's words intend to affect the audience to describe the challenges that Paul Tall faces as an "inner-city Native," while also referring to the marginalization of his people ("peeps").*
Cite a specific word or phrase from the text that supports your assertion and explain how it does so.	Cite a specific word or phrase from the text that supports your assertion and explain how it does so.
Tall Paul reflects on his challenging background/upbringing and the loss he feels from being an "inner-city Native" (i.e., "born with dim prospects, little peace in living/As a child hot headed 'bout the fact I wasn't wild"). Here, he is also somber about not being Native "enough," even if "wild" was a derogatory term used against his ancestors.	*When Tall Paul states "I was full of heat like a furnace 'cuz I wasn't furnished/With language and traditional ways of my peeps," he is referring to the decimation of his language and culture and his anger because of it.*

STUDENT WORKSHEET
Question: How does language give people power?

From the song **"Prayers in a Song" by Tall Paul**

Inner-city Native raised by bright lights, skyscrapers
Born with dim prospects, little peace in living
As a child, hot-headed 'bout the fact I wasn't wild
Like they called my ancestors, imagined what it'd be
To live nomadic off the land and free
Instead I was full of heat like a furnace 'cuz I wasn't furnished
With language and traditional ways of my peeps

1. How would you categorize the style of expression on display in the text above?

_____

2. Cite a piece of evidence from the text that supports your claim.

_____

_____

3. Explain the author's purpose behind choosing this style of expression for his words
(i.e., Who is Tall Paul's intended audience?).

_____

_____

4. Cite a piece of evidence from the text that supports your assertion.

_____

_____

5. Tall Paul says, "Like my ancestors, imagined what it'd be/To live nomadic off the land and free." In your own
words, explain what he means by this.

_____

_____

Tone is the author's attitude toward the subject.	**Mood** is the effect an author's words have on an audience (i.e., how the words make us feel).
What is Tall Paul's tone in the text above?	What mood has Tall Paul's lyric created in the audience in the text above?
_____	_____
_____	_____
_____	_____
Cite a specific word or phrase from the text that supports your assertion and explain how it does so.	Cite a specific word or phrase from the text that supports your assertion and explain how it does so.
_____	_____
_____	_____
_____	_____

LANGUAGE AND CONTEXT: ASSESSING STYLE, MEANING, AUDIENCE, AND WORD CHOICE
Question: How does language give people power?

Assignment: Describe the school's lunch

- In a text message.
- In a handwritten note that you'd pass to a friend.
- In a formal letter written to the principal.

Text #1:

John Student
Lynwood High School
4050 East Imperial Highway
Lynwood, CA 90262

Dear Mr. Principal,

It is with great regret that I wish to inform you about the lack of quality food being offered by our school's cafeteria. Simply put, I believe this matter requires an investigation.

As I am sure you know, student nutrition is a very serious issue. This is why I am not sure why our cafeteria is serving such substandard food. After all, plenty of studies have shown kids need high-quality nourishment to maintain their intellectual excellence throughout the day.

Being that you are a dedicated and thoughtful leader who always puts the best interests of the students at the top of his list, I look forward to a swift resolution to this pressing matter.

Sincerely,

John J. Student

Text #2:

Text #3:

Lnch @ dis skool ez WHACK!

INTERPRETATION GUIDE
Question: How does language give people power?

1. Identify the style of expression on display in Text 1 above.

a) Standard English b) Lunchtime English c) Text Message English

2. Provide a piece of textual evidence to support your answer.

The formal salutation, the correct use of headings, the proper grammar, the purposeful attention to subject verb agreement, and so on.

3. Explain the author's purpose behind choosing this style of expression to convey his or her message in Text 1.

There is a proper protocol when it comes to addressing someone (via a letter) in a position of authority. This is why the author uses standard English; it is the most appropriate form of writing a person ought to take if he or she wants to successfully reach his or her intended audience.

Cite 2 ADVANTAGES the author gains by using this style of expression	Cite 2 DISADVANTAGES possibly incurred by NOT USING this style of expression
1. *It shows respect for his or her audience.*	1. *His or her request might not be taken seriously.*
2. *Its appropriateness and politeness warrant a thoughtful response.*	2. *The author might be scoffed at or mocked for not knowing proper protocol.*

4. Identify the style of expression on display in Text 2 above.

a) Standard English **b)Lunchtime English** c) Text Message English

5. Provide a piece of textual evidence to support your answer choice.

The slang on the handwritten note, the lack of attention to grammar, the highly casual tone of the message, and so on.

6. Explain the author's purpose behind choosing this style of expression to convey his or her message in Text 2.

There is a proper protocol when it comes to addressing your peers/friends—especially when you are a student in school. This is why the author uses casual language that is fun and playful. Taken in context, it's entirely appropriate.

Cite 2 ADVANTAGES the author gains by using this style of expression	Cite 2 DISADVANTAGES possibly incurred by NOT USING this style of expression
1. *The reader will be receptive to the humor.*	1. *A violation of the unspoken code of notes.*
2. *Peers will read the message because it's in their vernacular.*	2. *To write a formal letter in the Queen's English to a friend might invite ridicule.*

7. Identify the style of expression on display in Text 3 above.

a) Standard English b)Lunchtime English **c) Text Message English**

8. Provide a piece of textual evidence to support your answer.

The dropping of vowels, the use of emoticons, the lack of regard for punctuation and grammar.

9. Explain the author's purpose behind choosing this style of expression to convey his or her message in Text 3.

There's a proper protocol when it comes to sending digital messages—particularly via social media. This is why the author uses language/a style that is apropos.

Cite 2 ADVANTAGES the author gains by using this style of expression	Cite 2 DISADVANTAGES possibly incurred by NOT USING this style of expression
1. *Proper context offers author credibility.*	1. *The audience will not read the message.*
2. *The audience will be more likely to read the message because it uses suitable shorthand.*	2. *The audience will view the author of the message as out of touch with protocol.*

STUDENT WORKSHEET
Question: How does language give people power?

1. Identify the style of expression on display in Text 1 above.

a) Standard English b)Lunchtime English c) Text Message English

2. Provide a piece of textual evidence to support your answer.

_____

_____

3. Explain the author's purpose behind choosing this style of expression to convey his or her message in Text 1.

_____

_____

Cite 2 ADVANTAGES the author gains by using this style of expression	Cite 2 DISADVANTAGES possibly incurred by NOT USING this style of expression
1. _____	1. _____
2.	2.

4. Identify the style of expression on display in Text 2 above.

a) Standard English b)Lunchtime English c) Text Message English

5. Provide a piece of textual evidence to support your answer.

_____

_____

6. Explain the author's purpose behind choosing this style of expression to convey his or her message in Text 2.

_____

_____

Cite 2 ADVANTAGES the author gains by using this style of expression	Cite 2 DISADVANTAGES possibly incurred by NOT USING this style of expression
1. _____	1. _____
2.	2.

7. Identify the style of expression on display in Text 3 above.

a) Standard English b)Lunchtime English c) Text Message English

8. Provide a piece of textual evidence to support your answer.

_____

_____

9. Explain the author's purpose behind choosing this style of expression to convey his or her message in Text 3.

_____

_____

Cite 2 ADVANTAGES the author gains by using this style of expression	Cite 2 DISADVANTAGES possibly incurred by NOT USING this style of expression
1. _____	1. _____
2.	2.

LANGUAGE AND CONTEXT: ASSESSING STYLE, MEANING, AUDIENCE, AND WORD CHOICE
Question: How does language give people power?

Five Thoughts on Language

1. Dictionaries aren't rulebooks. They follow language, they don't guide it.

"When it comes to correct English, there's no one in charge; the lunatics are running the asylum. The editors of a dictionary read a lot, keeping their eyes open for new words and senses that are used by many writers in many contexts, and the editors add or change the definitions accordingly.

"Should we follow rules as best we can? Do they make our writing better on average? Absolutely.

"But creative license is encouraged. Languages can, should and will change and that's great. To be a great writer, know the rules before you break them."
—THE SENSE OF STYLE: THE THINKING PERSON'S GUIDE TO WRITING IN THE 21ST CENTURY

2. There is no tribunal.

"There's no rules committee when it comes to English. It's not like the rules of Major League Baseball which are exactly what the rules committee stipulates them to be. That would just never work with language. There are hundreds of millions of English speakers and they are constantly adding new terms to the language. They're constantly changing shades of meaning.

"Do you want to live in a world where James Brown would be forced to sing 'I Feel Well' instead of 'I Feel Good'"? —STEVEN PRESSFIELD

3. From National Speech Week, 1917

In 1917, the National Council of Teachers of English prepared the following pledge for school students to recite in observance of National Speech Week:

I love the United States. I love my country's flag. I love my country's language. I promise:

1. That I will not dishonor my country's speech by leaving off the last syllable of words.

2. That I will say a good American "yes" and "no" in place of an Indian grunt "un-hum" and "nup-um" or a foreign "ya" or "yeh" and "nope."

3. That I will do my best to improve American speech by avoiding loud, rough tones, by enunciating distinctly, and by speaking pleasantly, clearly and sincerely.

4. That I will learn to articulate correctly as many words as possible during the year.

4. From eSchool News

"Just because they [students] use social media regularly in their daily lives doesn't mean they automatically know how to write in an academic setting online. They had to be taught that just because it [class] looks like Facebook does not mean it is Facebook. They can't 'LOL' and 'OMG' or use all lower-case letters and get credit in an online class. Academic situations require very different communication standards."
—RACHEL STOKES AND JAMES GARNER

5. Four hundred years ago, when black slaves were brought to America, Africans who spoke the same language were separated from each other. What we're seeing today, with this insane campaign to intimidate rappers and rap music, is just another form of separating people that speak a common language. —ICE CUBE

INTERPRETATION GUIDE
Question: How does language give people power?

Five Thoughts on Language

1. Identify two pieces of text, (out of the five provided,) that share a SIMILAR TONE.

Choice A) Answers will vary   Choice B) Could be 1 and 2 or 3 and 4

Cite two pieces of evidence, one from each text, that support your assertion above.

Choice A: Answers will vary	Choice B: Answers will vary
Textual Evidence: Answers will vary	Textual Evidence: Answers will vary

2. Identify two pieces of text, out of the five provided, that share a DISSIMILAR TONE.

Choice A) Answers will vary   Choice B) Could be 3 and 5 or 2 and 4 and/or 1

Cite two pieces of evidence, one from each text, that support your assertion above.

Choice A: Answers will vary	Choice B: Answers will vary
Textual Evidence: Answers will vary	Textual Evidence: Answers will vary

3. In your estimation, out of the five selections provided, which piece of text makes the STRONGEST argument?

- Answers will vary, most probably among all except 3

Cite a piece of evidence from the text that supports your assertion.

Textual Evidence: Answers will vary _____

4. In your estimation, out of the five selections provided, which piece of text makes the WEAKEST argument?

- Most probably will be 3, but answers may vary.

Cite a piece of evidence from the text that supports your assertion.

Textual Evidence: The evidence will most probably point to all of the dictates, which seem so archaic (such as the "Yeh" or "Nope" or "Indian grunt" or avoiding "loud, rough tones").

5. Identify the mood created by each of the five texts, and cite a word or phrase from each piece you feel MOST HELPED TO CONTRIBUTE to the creation of this mood.

Dictionaries aren't rulebooks	There is no tribunal	National Speech Week, 1917	From eSchool News	Four hundred years ago
Mood: *Informed and permissive*	Mood: *Rebellious and fed up*	Mood: *A sense of being ridiculous*	Mood: *Invokes respect for protocol*	Mood: *Anger/ great displeasure*
Key Word or phrase: *"Languages can, should and will change."*	Key Word or phrase: *"There's no rules committee when it comes to English."*	Key Word or phrase: *Pretty much the whole thing*	Key Word or phrase: *"They can't 'LOL' and 'OMG'… in an online class."*	Key Word or phrase: *"Africans who spoke the same language were separated."*

STUDENT WORKSHEET
Question: How does language give people power?

Five Thoughts on Language

1. Identify two pieces of text, out of the five provided, that share a SIMILAR TONE.

Choice A) _____ Choice B) _____

Cite two pieces of evidence, one from each text, that support your assertion above.

Choice A:	Choice B:
Textual Evidence: _____	Textual Evidence: _____

2. Identify two pieces of text, out of the five provided, that share a DISSIMILAR TONE.

Choice A) _____ Choice B) _____

Cite two pieces of evidence, one from each text, that support your assertion above.

Choice A:	Choice B:
Textual Evidence: _____	Textual Evidence: _____

3. In your estimation, out of the five selections provided, which piece of text makes the STRONGEST argument?

_____

Cite a piece of evidence from the text that supports your assertion.

Textual Evidence: _____

_____

4. In your estimation, out of the five selections provided, which piece of text makes the WEAKEST argument?

_____

Cite a piece of evidence from the text that supports your assertion.

Textual Evidence: _____

_____

5. Identify the mood created by each of the five texts, and cite a word or phrase from each piece you feel MOST HELPED TO CONTRIBUTE to the creation of this mood.

Dictionaries aren't rulebooks	There is no tribunal	National Speech Week, 1917	From eSchool News	Four hundred years ago
Mood:	Mood:	Mood:	Mood:	Mood:
_____	_____	_____	_____	_____
Key Word or phrase:	Key Word or phrase:	Key Word or phrase:	Key Word or phrase:	Key Word or phrase:
_____	_____	_____	_____	_____

OPEN MIC: PUTTING THE QUESTION TO YOU!

*Please answer the question below making sure that you
use textual evidence to support whatever claims(s) you assert.*

In your opinion, is violence an appropriate solution for resolving conflict?

_____
_____
_____
_____
_____
_____
_____
_____
_____
_____
_____
_____
_____
_____
_____
_____
_____
_____
_____
_____
_____
_____

UNIT 6
ANALYZING THEMES: COMPARING AND CONTRASTING TEXT

Essential Question

Is my cultural category my identity?

Voices in the unit

Sherman Alexie
Litefoot
Christopher Hitchens
Chuck D
Bambu
Philip Vera Cruz
MC Jin
Seung Won Kim
Duende
Gloria E. Anzaldúa

Junot Díaz
Immortal Technique
Malcolm X
Styles P
James Owen
Sa-Roc
Alice Walker
Jay-Z
Jane Austen
Kendrick Lamar

Standards-Based Literacy Skills Targeted:

Identifying Common Themes Between Disparate Texts
Providing Textual Evidence to Support Assertions
Recognizing Compositional Similarities
Distinguishing Stylistic Differences
Rendering Opinions
Providing Evidence-Based Reasoning to Support Assertions
Reading Closely
Writing: Making Claims and Providing Evidence

INTERPRETATION GUIDE
Question: Is my cultural category my identity?

Consider the following two texts…

Text 1

From the song "MY LAND" by LITEFOOT
Now I'm a make it all fair again
If you ain't a Indian, fool, then you really ain't American
The cavalry celebrated victory and glory
I read it! It's history! Nah, it's his story
Picture a beautiful country with green trees
Living in peace—you see thousands of teepees
Living off the land and our own laws
No presidents, deficit, or government flaws
But now our people are living in poverty
And they taught us a word they called property

Text 2

From *The Absolutely True Diary of a Part-Time Indian*,
Sherman Alexie's young adult novel

"We Indians have lost everything. We lost our native land, we lost our languages, we lost our songs and dances. We lost each other. We only know how to lose and be lost."

1. Identify a common theme that runs through the texts.

   Note: Answers may vary.

   - The loss of land, culture, and language of First Nation people (Native Americans)

2. Cite a piece of textual evidence from Text 1 that supports the assertion you made above (in question #1).
   - Litefoot's statement "But now our people are living in poverty/And they taught us the word they called property" supports this claim, as well as most of the text references to the rewriting of history.

3. Cite a piece of textual evidence from Text 2 that supports the assertion you made above (in question #1).
   - Sherman Alexie's statement that "We have lost everything" and the whole text supports this claim.

4. In what way are the authors similar in their approach to the subject matter?
   - Both authors are similar because they address what Native American's lost at the hands of the U.S. occupation.
   - Both authors make direct reference to their land.

5. In what way are the authors different in their approach to the subject matter?
   - Litefoot uses impassioned and specific language; Alexie is concise and somber.
   - Litefoot makes direct and specific references to history (his story), Calvary, and the government impositions on his people; Alexie makes a more broad and sweeping allusion to overall loss and how it has affected his people ("We lost each other").
   - Litefoot tells a story about the effects of U.S. history on the traditions of his people; Alexie speaks about how the loss has affected his people personally.

6. In your opinion, which text does a superior job of communicating the author's main idea?
   Explain why (making sure to cite a piece of textual evidence to support your answer).

Possible replies; answers may vary.

Why Litefoot is superior	Why Alexie is superior
Litefoot is more expansive and specific, using many examples to support his points and referring to a before and after scenario of his people.	Alexie is more straightforward, speaking in a direct, concise manner. The whole piece of text serves as evidence.

STUDENT WORKSHEET
Question: Is my cultural category my identity?

Consider the following two texts…

Text 1	**Text 2**
From the song "MY LAND" by LITEFOOT Now I'm a make it all fair again If you ain't a Indian, fool, then you really ain't American The cavalry celebrated victory and glory I read it! It's history! Nah, it's his story Picture a beautiful country with green trees Living in peace—you see thousands of teepees Living off the land and our own laws No presidents, deficit, or government flaws But now our people are living in poverty And they taught us a word they called property	From *The Absolutely True Diary of a Part-Time Indian*, Sherman Alexie's young adult novel "We Indians have lost everything. We lost our native land, we lost our languages, we lost our songs and dances. We lost each other. We only know how to lose and be lost."

1. Identify a common theme that runs through the texts.

_____

_____

2. Cite a piece of textual evidence from Text 1 that supports the assertion you made above (in question #1).

_____

_____

3. Cite a piece of textual evidence from Text 2 that supports the assertion you made above (in question #1).

_____

_____

4. In what way are the authors similar in their approach to the subject matter?

_____

_____

5. In what way are the authors different in their approach to the subject matter?

_____

_____

6. In your opinion, which text does a superior job of communicating the author's main idea?
Explain why (making sure to cite a piece of textual evidence to support your answer).

_____

_____

INTERPRETATION GUIDE
Question: Is my cultural category my identity?

Consider the following two texts…

Text 1

"For years, I declined to fill in the form for my Senate press credential that asked me to state my 'race,' unless I was permitted to put 'human.' The form had to be completed under penalty of perjury, so I could not in conscience put 'white,' which is not even a color let alone a 'race,' and I sternly declined to put 'Caucasian,' which is an exploded term from a discredited ethnology. Surely the essential and unarguable core of MLK's campaign was the insistence that pigmentation was a false measure of mankind."

—CHRISTOPHER HITCHENS

Text 2

"People are so confused about race and hip-hop that people didn't even consider the Beastie Boys one of the greatest rap groups of all time because they were white."

—CHUCK D

1. Identify a common theme that runs through the texts.
   Note: Answers may vary.
   - The color of a person's skin affects the way a person is seen by society.

2. Cite a piece of textual evidence from Text 1 that supports the assertion you made above (in question #1).
   - Hitchens statement "the essential and unarguable core of MLK's campaign was the insistence that pigmentation was a false measure of mankind" supports this claim.

3. Cite a piece of textual evidence from Text 2 that supports the assertion you made above (in question #1).
   - Chuck D's statement that the Beastie Boys never got their proper due from the hip-hop community "because they were white" supports this claim.

4. In what way are the authors similar in their approach to the subject matter?
   - Both authors are similar because they address how different aspects of our culture show [unnecessary] prejudice.
   - Both authors make an allusion to someone else to drive home their point.
   - Both authors speak about white people.

5. In what way are the authors different in their approach to the subject matter?
   - Hitchens uses formal, ornate language; Chuck D is concise and direct.
   - Chuck D makes a reference to a musical group; Hitchens makes a reference to a political figure.
   - Hitchens tells a story about his own experience; Chuck D speaks about the experience of his contemporaries.

6. In your opinion, which text does a superior job of communicating the author's main idea?
   Explain why (making sure to cite textual evidence to support your answer).

Possible replies; answers may vary.

Why Hitchens is superior	Why Chuck D is superior
Hitchens is more expansive and eloquent, using many more big words such as "ethnology" and "unarguable" to make his point.	Chuck D is more straightforward, speaking in a direct, concise manner (i.e., less is more). The whole piece of text serves as evidence.

STUDENT WORKSHEET

Question: Is my cultural category my identity?

Consider the following two texts…

Text 1

"For years, I declined to fill in the form for my Senate press credential that asked me to state my 'race,' unless I was permitted to put 'human.' The form had to be completed under penalty of perjury, so I could not in conscience put 'white,' which is not even a color let alone a 'race,' and I sternly declined to put 'Caucasian,' which is an exploded term from a discredited ethnology. Surely the essential and unarguable core of MLK's campaign was the insistence that pigmentation was a false measure of mankind."

—CHRISTOPHER HITCHENS

Text 2

"People are so confused about race and hip-hop that people didn't even consider the Beastie Boys one of the greatest rap groups of all time because they were white."

—CHUCK D

1. Identify a common theme that runs through the texts.

_____

_____

2. Cite a piece of textual evidence from Text 1 that supports the assertion you made above (in question #1).

_____

_____

3. Cite a piece of textual evidence from Text 2 that supports the assertion you made above (in question #1).

_____

_____

4. In what way are the authors similar in their approach to the subject matter?

_____

_____

5. In what way are the authors different in their approach to the subject matter?

_____

_____

6. In your opinion, which text does a superior job of communicating the author's main idea? Explain why (making sure to cite a piece of textual evidence to support your answer).

_____

_____

INTERPRETATION GUIDE
Question: Is my cultural category my identity?

Consider the following two texts…

Text 1

From the song "OROSI" by BAMBU
Before the farm workers united, the people united
The grape strikes for the Mexican farmers just seemed right
So they joined the Filipinos and a bond was born
When manong Philip Vera Cruz and uncle Larry Itliong
Took on the task needed to get the farmers even
Watching brown hands digging 'til their fingers bleeding
So they marched in March of '66 in Delano
One foot in front of the other until Sacramento
Just to get the wages they deserve
The treatment they deserve, the people get served

Text 2

"I could not be concerned just about myself or my family but also of the people who are like me. That's why I got involved. It was the union that really brought me about. If you are alone, what can you do? When you build unity, you cannot build unity without others. You can't just think about yourself. You'll be too weak. You're not big enough to carry the load; you need everybody."

—PHILIP VERA CRUZ, FILIPINO AMERICAN LABOR LEADER, COFOUNDER OF THE UNITED FARM WORKERS

1. Identify a common theme that runs through the texts.
- A people united can move mountains and change the world.
- Sometimes we all must look past our own individual needs to work for the betterment of all.

2. Cite a piece of textual evidence from Text 1 that supports the assertion you made above (in question #1).
- Bambu's statement "Just to get the wages they deserve/The treatment they deserve, the people get served" supports this claim.

3. Cite a piece of textual evidence from Text 2 that supports the assertion you made above (in question #1).
- Vera Cruz's statement "If you are alone, what can you do?" supports this claim.

4. In what way are the authors similar in their approach to the subject matter?
- The authors are similar because they address the need for fairness.
- The authors make an allusion to their own kind to drive home their point.
- The authors' words speak to the power and need for social justice.

5. In what way are the authors different in their approach to the subject matter?
- Bambu uses specific, historically rooted language; Vera Cruz is more nonspecific.
- Bambu makes a reference to specific movements for equality (i.e., the farm workers united/Mexican and Filipino); Vera Cruz speaks broadly for all people.
- Bambu tells a historical story with a direct reference to Vera Cruz; Vera Cruz speaks about the general beliefs that inform his work.

6. In your opinion, which text does a superior job of communicating the author's main idea?
Explain why (making sure to cite a piece of textual evidence to support your answer).

Possible replies; answers may vary.

Why Bambu is superior	Why Vera Cruz is superior
Bambu is more expansive and specifically highlights the movement for equality that Mexican and Filipino farm workers embarked upon to make his point.	Vera Cruz is more straightforward, speaking in a direct, concise manner to share his personal belief about unity, as evidenced by lines such as "You can't just think about yourself. You'll be too weak."

STUDENT WORKSHEET
Question: Is my cultural category my identity?

Consider the following two texts...

Text 1

From the song "OROSI" by BAMBU
Before the farm workers united, the people united
The grape strikes for the Mexican farmers just seemed right
So they joined the Filipinos and a bond was born
When manong Philip Vera Cruz and uncle Larry Itliong
Took on the task needed to get the farmers even
Watching brown hands digging 'til their fingers bleeding
So they marched in March of '66 in Delano
One foot in front of the other until Sacramento
Just to get the wages they deserve
The treatment they deserve, the people get served

Text 2

"I could not be concerned just about myself or my family but also of the people who are like me. That's why I got involved. It was the union that really brought me about. If you are alone, what can you do? When you build unity, you cannot build unity without others. You can't just think about yourself. You'll be too weak. You're not big enough to carry the load; you need everybody."

—PHILIP VERA CRUZ, FILIPINO AMERICAN LABOR LEADER, COFOUNDER OF THE UNITED FARM WORKERS

1. Identify a common theme that runs through the texts.

_____

_____

2. Cite a piece of textual evidence from Text 1 that supports the assertion you made above (in question #1).

_____

_____

3. Cite a piece of textual evidence from Text 2 that supports the assertion you made above (in question #1).

_____

_____

4. In what way are the authors similar in their approach to the subject matter?

_____

_____

5. In what way are the authors different in their approach to the subject matter?

_____

_____

6. In your opinion, which text does a superior job of communicating the author's main idea? Explain why (making sure to cite a piece of textual evidence to support your answer).

_____

_____

INTERPRETATION GUIDE

Question: Is my cultural category my identity?

Consider the following two texts...

Text 1

From the song "CHINESE NEW YEAR" by MC JIN
Every Sunday
It was part of the tradition
While y'all was at church
Dimsum was our religion
I'm on a quest for love
That's just part of my pursuits
No matter where I go
I'm always stickin' to my roots

Text 2

"I wondered how Asian-Americans think about their identities. Do they feel discriminated when people call them Koreans or Chinese just because of their races? Or do they really consider themselves as Asians? After asking these questions to several Asian-American friends, I realized the necessity of a cultural institution for second and third generation immigrants who want to find their roots."

—SEUNG WON KIM

1. Identify a common theme that runs through the texts.
- A common theme is the need to connect to one's roots.
- Both texts reflect on Asian identity.

2. Cite a piece of textual evidence from Text 1 that supports the assertion you made above (in question #1).
- MC Jin's statement "No matter where I go/I'm always stickin' to my roots" supports this claim.

3. Cite a piece of textual evidence from Text 2 that supports the assertion you made above (in question #1).
- Won Kim's statement "I realized the necessity of a cultural institution for second and third generation immigrants who want to find their roots" supports this claim.

4. In what way are the authors similar in their approach to the subject matter?
- The authors are similar because they address the need to connect to their past.
- The authors make an allusion to tradition and/or cultural institutions to support their need for cultural connection.

5. In what way are the authors different in their approach to the subject matter?
- MC Jin uses direct, playful language; Won Kim is nuanced and exploratory.
- MC Jin makes a direct reference to his tradition; Won Kim makes a reference to the need for a cultural institution.
- MC Jin tells a story about his own experience and is proud of his roots; Won Kim speaks about the experience of Asian Americans and how they may feel discriminated against because of their identity.

6. In your opinion, which text does a superior job of communicating the author's main idea? Explain why (making sure to cite a piece of textual evidence to support your answer).

Possible replies; answers may vary.

Why MC Jin is superior	Why Won Kim is superior
Jin is more direct about his tradition and needs to stay connected to his past, as evidenced by lines such as "No matter where I go/I'm always stickin' to my roots."	Won Kim is more nuanced, exploring how identity can be discriminated against, as evidenced by such lines as "I realized the necessity of a cultural institution for second and third generation immigrants."

STUDENT WORKSHEET
Question: Is my cultural category my identity?

Consider the following two texts…

Text 1

From the song "CHINESE NEW YEAR" by MC JIN
Every Sunday
It was part of the tradition
While y'all was at church
Dimsum was our religion
I'm on a quest for love
That's just part of my pursuits
No matter where I go
I'm always stickin' to my roots

Text 2

I wondered how Asian-Americans think about their identities. Do they feel discriminated when people call them Koreans or Chinese just because of their races? Or do they really consider themselves as Asians? After asking these questions to several Asian-American friends, I realized the necessity of a cultural institution for second and third generation immigrants who want to find their roots.

—SEUNG WON KIM

1. Identify a common theme that runs through the texts.

_____

_____

2. Cite a piece of textual evidence from Text 1 that supports the assertion you made above (in question #1).

_____

_____

3. Cite a piece of textual evidence from Text 2 that supports the assertion you made above (in question #1).

_____

_____

4. In what way are the authors similar in their approach to the subject matter?

_____

_____

5. In what way are the authors different in their approach to the subject matter?

_____

_____

6. In your opinion, which text does a superior job of communicating the author's main idea?
Explain why (making sure to cite a piece of textual evidence to support your answer).

_____

_____

INTERPRETATION GUIDE
Question: Is my cultural category my identity?

Consider the following two texts…

Text 1

From the song "CHICANO RAP" by DUENDE
Chicano Rap is for the people that have been through that pain
It's for the one that wants to put a hollow point through his brain
The limit is the sky we can't make it over night
But eventually we might we just gotta do it right
Chicano Rap is for the ones that always show love
So what we do it to show love back
Chicano Rap is for the Brown Pride

Text 2

"So, if you want to really hurt me, talk badly about my language. Ethnic identity is twin skin to linguistic identity—I am my language. Until I can take pride in my language, I cannot take pride in myself. Until I can accept as legitimate Chicano Texas Spanish, Tex-Mex and all the other languages I speak, I cannot accept the legitimacy of myself."

—GLORIA E. ANZALDÚA

---

1. Identify a common theme that runs through the texts.
   - One common theme is how it's important to take pride in one's self and culture.
   - Both pieces talk about pain and hurt.

2. Cite a piece of textual evidence from Text 1 that supports the assertion you made above (in question #1).
   - Duende's statement "Chicano Rap is for the ones that always show love/So what we do it to show love back/Chicano Rap is for the Brown Pride" supports this claim.

3. Cite a piece of textual evidence from Text 2 that supports the assertion you made above (in question #1).
   - Anzaldúa's statement "Until I can take pride in my language, I cannot take pride in myself" supports this claim.

4. In what way are the authors similar in their approach to the subject matter?
   - The authors are similar because they address pride and identity.
   - The authors make an allusion to being Chicano.
   - The authors speak about, or make allusions to, as Anzaldúa put it, "the legitimacy of self."

5. In what way are the authors different in their approach to the subject matter?
   - Duende uses simple, direct language; Anzaldúa is complex and nuanced.
   - Duende makes a reference to his people; Anzaldúa makes a reference to her personal identity.
   - Duende tells a story about his people; Anzaldúa speaks about her own experience.

6. In your opinion, which text does a superior job of communicating the author's main idea?
   Explain why (making sure to cite a piece of textual evidence to support your answer).

Possible replies; answers may vary.

Why Duende is superior	Why Anzaldúa is superior
Duende's song is is superior because it's a general anthem of pride for his culture, as evidenced by the line "Chicano Rap is for the people that have been through that pain."	Anzaldúa is more specific and nuanced and deals directly with her own personal experience, as evidenced by the very direct and personal "I am my language."

STUDENT WORKSHEET

Question: Is my cultural category my identity?

Consider the following two texts…

Text 1

From the song "CHICANO RAP" by DUENDE
Chicano Rap is for the people that have been through that pain
It's for the one that wants to put a hollow point through his brain
The limit is the sky we can't make it over night
But eventually we might we just gotta do it right
Chicano Rap is for the ones that always show love
So what we do it to show love back
Chicano Rap is for the Brown Pride

Text 2

"So, if you want to really hurt me, talk badly about my language. Ethnic identity is twin skin to linguistic identity—I am my language. Until I can take pride in my language, I cannot take pride in myself. Until I can accept as legitimate Chicano Texas Spanish, Tex-Mex and all the other languages I speak, I cannot accept the legitimacy of myself."

—GLORIA E. ANZALDÚA

1. Identify a common theme that runs through the texts.

_____

_____

2. Cite a piece of textual evidence from Text 1 that supports the assertion you made above (in question #1).

_____

_____

3. Cite a piece of textual evidence from Text 2 that supports the assertion you made above (in question #1).

_____

_____

4. In what way are the authors similar in their approach to the subject matter?

_____

_____

5. In what way are the authors different in their approach to the subject matter?

_____

_____

6. In your opinion, which text does a superior job of communicating the author's main idea? Explain why (making sure to cite a piece of textual evidence to support your answer).

_____

_____

INTERPRETATION GUIDE

Question: Is my cultural category my identity?

Consider the following two texts…

Text 1

"We all know that there are language forms that are considered impolite and out of order, no matter what truths these languages might be carrying. If you talk with a harsh, urbanized accent and you use too many profanities, that will often get you barred from many arenas, no matter what you're trying to say. On the other hand, polite, formal language is allowed almost anywhere even when all it is communicating is hatred and violence. Power always privileges its own discourse while marginalizing those who would challenge it or that are the victims of its power."

—JUNOT DÍAZ

Text 2

From the song "ULTIMAS PALABRAS" by IMMORTAL TECHNIQUE

"My words, of course, will be marginalized, demonized in typical fashion. Any time you dare to question the power structure they say you hate America. No, I love this country. I see its beauty every day in its people. And I love it a lot more than those who have abandoned the American worker that have chosen to exploit and try to take away every single benefit she has, those that attempt to make excuses for every atrocity committed, in the name of supposed freedom."

1. Identify a common theme that runs through the texts.
   - They both address the relationship between language and power.
   - They both speak to the idea of power through words and speech.

2. Cite a piece of textual evidence from Text 1 that supports the assertion you made above (in question #1).
   - Junot Díaz's statement "Power always privileges its own discourse while marginalizing those who would challenge it or that are the victims of its power" supports this claim.

3. Cite a piece of textual evidence from Text 2 that supports the assertion you made above (in question #1).
   - Immortal Technique's statement "My words, of course,/will be marginalized, demonized,/in typical fashion,/ Anytime you dare to question the power structure they say you hate America" supports this claim.

4. In what way are the authors similar in their approach to the subject matter?
   - The authors are similar because they address how power/power structure influences language.
   - The authors make an allusion to perception and how they and/or people are perceived because of the language they use and its content.

5. In what way are the authors different in their approach to the subject matter?
   - Immortal Technique uses specific, impassioned language; Junot Díaz makes a point that is generalized to include all people.
   - Immortal Technique makes reference to his own experience and how he is perceived; Junot Díaz makes a reference to how other people are perceived.
   - Immortal Technique tells about being marginalized because of what he says; Junot Díaz speaks about being marginalized because of how people speak.

6. In your opinion, which text does a superior job of communicating the author's main idea? Explain why (making sure to cite textual evidence to support your answer).

Possible replies; answers may vary.

Why Junot Diaz is superior	Why Immortal Technique is superior
Junot Díaz is more expansive, speaking in direct examples about how people are treated because of *how* they speak, as evidenced by the phrase "We all know that there are language forms that are considered impolite and out of order."	Immortal Technique is more passionate in describing his own experience and how he is misinterpreted because of how he chooses to use his language, as evidenced by the phrase "My words, of course, will be marginalized."

STUDENT WORKSHEET
Question: Is my cultural category my identity?

Consider the following two texts…

Text 1

"We all know that there are language forms that are considered impolite and out of order, no matter what truths these languages might be carrying. If you talk with a harsh, urbanized accent and you use too many profanities, that will often get you barred from many arenas, no matter what you're trying to say. On the other hand, polite, formal language is allowed almost anywhere even when all it is communicating is hatred and violence. Power always privileges its own discourse while marginalizing those who would challenge it or that are the victims of its power."

—JUNOT DÍAZ

Text 2

From the song "ULTIMAS PALABRAS" by IMMORTAL TECHNIQUE

"My words, of course, will be marginalized, demonized in typical fashion. Any time you dare to question the power structure they say you hate America. No, I love this country. I see its beauty every day in its people. And I love it a lot more than those who have abandoned the American worker that have chosen to exploit and try to take away every single benefit she has, those that attempt to make excuses for every atrocity committed, in the name of supposed freedom."

1. Identify a common theme that runs through the texts.

_____

_____

2. Cite a piece of textual evidence from Text 1 that supports the assertion you made above (in question #1).

_____

_____

3. Cite a piece of textual evidence from Text 2 that supports the assertion you made above (in question #1).

_____

_____

4. In what way are the authors similar in their approach to the subject matter?

_____

_____

5. In what way are the authors different in their approach to the subject matter?

_____

_____

6. In your opinion, which text does a superior job of communicating the author's main idea? Explain why (making sure to cite a piece of textual evidence to support your answer).

_____

_____

INTERPRETATION GUIDE
Question: Is my cultural category my identity?

Consider the following two texts...

Text 1

"We're not Americans, we're Africans who happen to be in America. We were kidnapped and brought here against our will from Africa. We didn't land on Plymouth Rock—that rock landed on us."

—MALCOLM X

Text 2

From the song "RISING DOWN" by STYLES P WITH THE ROOTS AND MOS DEF
I'm an African-American
they sell drugs in the hood but the man, he move the medicine...
You know I'm hip to it and its hard to claim the land
When my great great great grands were shipped to it

1. Identify a common theme that runs through the texts.

Note: Answers may vary.

- The reluctance to claim an "American" identity when Africans were brought to America as slaves.

2. Cite a piece of textual evidence from Text 1 that supports the assertion you made above (in question #1).
- Malcolm X's statement "We were kidnapped and brought here against our will from Africa" supports this claim.

3. Cite a piece of textual evidence from Text 2 that supports the assertion you made above (in question #1).
- Styles P's statement "it's hard to claim the land when my great great great grands were shipped to it" supports this claim.

4. In what way are the authors similar in their approach to the subject matter?
- The authors are similar because they address how the history of slavery makes them reluctant to claim an "American" identity.
- The authors make allusions to America or being an American.
- The authors speak about the concept of "African-American."

5. In what way are the authors different in their approach to the subject matter?
- Malcolm X uses charged, clear language; Styles P uses a styled approach to make his point.
- Styles P prefaces his statement with an allusion to the current situation in the "hood" vs. "the man," which is representative of American capitalism; Malcolm X makes a reference to a historical touch point, Plymouth Rock.
- Styles P tells a story about his own experience; Malcolm X speaks to the historical reality that informs his experience.

6. In your opinion, which text does a superior job of communicating the author's main idea?
Explain why (making sure to cite a piece of textual evidence to support your answer).

Possible replies; answers may vary.

Why Malcolm X is superior	Why Styles P is superior
Malcolm X uses passionate and blunt references to the historic tragedy of slavery. He speaks to the "how" of African descendants in America and implies his anger at it.	Styles P is more rooted in the current situation, with the "hood" vs. "the man" reference, while also alluding to historical information, which informs his reluctance to claim the "American" in African-American.

STUDENT WORKSHEET
Question: Is my cultural category my identity?

Consider the following two texts...

Text 1

"We're not Americans, we're Africans who happen to be in America. We were kidnapped and brought here against our will from Africa. We didn't land on Plymouth Rock—that rock landed on us."

—MALCOLM X

Text 2

From the song "RISING DOWN" by STYLES P WITH THE ROOTS AND MOS DEF
I'm an African-American
they sell drugs in the hood but the man, he move the medicine...
You know I'm hip to it and its hard to claim the land
When my great great great grands were shipped to it

1. Identify a common theme that runs through the texts.

2. Cite a piece of textual evidence from Text 1 that supports the assertion you made above (in question #1).

3. Cite a piece of textual evidence from Text 2 that supports the assertion you made above (in question #1).

4. In what way are the authors similar in their approach to the subject matter?

5. In what way are the authors different in their approach to the subject matter?

6. In your opinion, which text does a superior job of communicating the author's main idea? Explain why (making sure to cite a piece of textual evidence to support your answer).

INTERPRETATION GUIDE
Question: Is my cultural category my identity?

Consider the following two texts…

Text 1

"The new data supports the single origin, or 'out of Africa' theory for anatomically modern humans, which says that these early humans colonized the planet after spreading out of the continent some 50,000 years ago."

—JAMES OWEN, NATIONAL GEOGRAPHIC

Text 2

From the song "BLACK GOD THEORY" by SA-ROC
Just call me the one but I'm not one to mess with
Genetic engineered you, took one egg to make your flesh with
Held the masterpiece then stamped my name with double exes
Formed your whole world and on the 7th day I rested

---

1. Identify a common theme that runs through the texts.

Note: Answers may vary.

- These statements explore origins and the creation story, rooted in Africa.

2. Cite a piece of textual evidence from Text 1 that supports the assertion you made above (in question #1).
- James Owen's statement "The new data supports the single origin, or 'out of Africa' theory for anatomically modern humans" supports this claim.

3. Cite a piece of textual evidence from Text 2 that supports the assertion you made above (in question #1).
- Sa-Roc's statements "Just call me the one" and "Formed your whole world and on the 7th day I rested" support this claim.

4. In what way are the authors similar in their approach to the subject matter?
- The authors are similar because they speak about origin/creation stories.
- The authors make an allusion to African or blackness (Owen "out of Africa" and Sa-Roc's "Black god theory").
- The authors speak about science.

5. In what way are the authors different in their approach to the subject matter?
- Owen uses specific, scientific, theoretical language; Sa-Roc's song is a hyperbolic creation story.
- Owen makes a specific scientific reference to human origin; Sa-Roc makes references to genetic creation and world creation.

6. In your opinion, which text does a superior job of communicating the author's main idea? Explain why (making sure to cite a piece of textual evidence to support your answer).

Possible replies; answers may vary.

Why Owen is superior	Why Sa-Roc is superior
His statement is grounded in specific scientific findings.	Sa-Roc is more biological, hyperbolic, and profound, as she claims to be responsible for all of "god's" creation. This is also an affirming stance of the power of women (i.e., the chromosome references).

STUDENT WORKSHEET

Question: Is my cultural category my identity?

Consider the following two texts…

Text 1

"The new data supports the single origin, or 'out of Africa' theory for anatomically modern humans, which says that these early humans colonized the planet after spreading out of the continent some 50,000 years ago."

—JAMES OWEN, NATIONAL GEOGRAPHIC

Text 2

From the song "BLACK GOD THEORY" by SA-ROC
Just call me the one but I'm not one to mess with
Genetic engineered you, took one egg to make your flesh with
Held the masterpiece then stamped my name with double exes
Formed your whole world and on the 7th day I rested

1. Identify a common theme that runs through the texts.

_____

_____

2. Cite a piece of textual evidence from Text 1 that supports the assertion you made above (in question #1).

_____

_____

3. Cite a piece of textual evidence from Text 2 that supports the assertion you made above (in question #1).

_____

_____

4. In what way are the authors similar in their approach to the subject matter?

_____

_____

5. In what way are the authors different in their approach to the subject matter?

_____

_____

6. In your opinion, which text does a superior job of communicating the author's main idea? Explain why (making sure to cite a piece of textual evidence to support your answer).

_____

_____

INTERPRETATION GUIDE
Question: Is my cultural category my identity?

Consider the following two texts…

Text 1	Text 2
"Helped are those who love all the colors of all the human beings, as they love all the colors of the animals and plants; none of their children, nor any of their ancestors, nor any parts of themselves, shall be hidden from them." —ALICE WALKER	"I think hip-hop has done more for racial relations than most cultural icons…You see it all the time. Go to any club. People are intermingling, hanging out, having fun, enjoying the same music. Everywhere you go, people are listening to hip-hop and partying together. Hip-hop has done that." —JAY-Z

1. Identify a common theme that runs through the texts.
Note: Answers may vary.
- Both of these statements expound on racial equity.

2. Cite a piece of textual evidence from Text 1 that supports the assertion you made above (in question #1).
- Jay-Z's statement "I think hip-hop has done more for racial relations than most cultural icons" supports this claim.

3. Cite a piece of textual evidence from Text 2 that supports the assertion you made above (in question #1).
- Alice Walker's statement "Helped are those who love all colors of the human beings" supports this claim.

4. In what way are the authors similar in their approach to the subject matter?
- The authors are similar because they speak about race relations.
- The authors make an allusion to unity (Walker, "all the human beings," and Jay Z, "People are intermingling").

5. In what way are the authors different in their approach to the subject matter?
- Walker uses general, aspirational language; Jay-Z uses specific examples.
- Walker makes a case for being oneself and not hiding any part of oneself; Jay-Z makes references to hip-hop creating the space for people to express themselves.

6. In your opinion, which text does a superior job of communicating the author's main idea?
Explain why (making sure to cite a piece of textual evidence to support your answer).

Possible replies; answers may vary.

Why Walker is superior	Why Jay-Z is superior
Walker's statement is inspirational and aspirational and speaks to an ideal that will create unity/equality.	Jay-Z is more specific, as he claims hip-hop to be a catalyst to racial equity and unity.

STUDENT WORKSHEET
Question: Is my cultural category my identity?

Consider the following two texts...

Text 1

"Helped are those who love all the colors of all the human beings, as they love all the colors of the animals and plants; none of their children, nor any of their ancestors, nor any parts of themselves, shall be hidden from them."

—ALICE WALKER

Text 2

I think hip-hop has done more for racial relations than most cultural icons...You see it all the time. Go to any club. People are intermingling, hanging out, having fun, enjoying the same music. Everywhere you go, people are listening to hip-hop and partying together. Hip-hop has done that."

—JAY-Z

1. Identify a common theme that runs through the texts.

_____

_____

2. Cite a piece of textual evidence from Text 1 that supports the assertion you made above (in question #1).

_____

_____

3. Cite a piece of textual evidence from Text 2 that supports the assertion you made above (in question #1).

_____

_____

4. In what way are the authors similar in their approach to the subject matter?

_____

_____

5. In what way are the authors different in their approach to the subject matter?

_____

_____

6. In your opinion, which text does a superior job of communicating the author's main idea? Explain why (making sure to cite a piece of textual evidence to support your answer).

_____

_____

INTERPRETATION GUIDE
Question: Is my cultural category my identity?

Consider the following two texts…

Text 1	Text 2
"Our scars make us know that our past was for real." —JANE AUSTEN	From the song "I" by KENDRICK LAMAR I wear my heart on my sleeve, let the runway start You know the miserable do love company What do you want from me and my scars? Everybody lack confidence, everybody lack confidence How many times my potential was anonymous? How many times the city making me promises? So I promise this I love myself

1. Identify a common theme that runs through the texts.
- One theme is regardless of your cultural category everyone holds hurt from his or her past.
- Another theme is that pain is not always a bad thing.

2. Cite a piece of textual evidence from Text 1 that supports the assertion you made above (in question #1).
- Jane Austen's entire quote supports this claim.

3. Cite a piece of textual evidence from Text 2 that supports the assertion you made above (in question #1).
- Kendrick Lamar's statement "How many times the city making me promises?" supports this claim because these words imply hurtful disappointment.

4. In what way are the authors similar in their approach to the subject matter?
- The authors are similar because they attest to the positive power of hurt.
- The authors are reflective about the past and how it shapes the present.

5. In what way are the authors different in their approach to the subject matter?
- Jane Austen is concise; Kendrick Lamar is more flowery and expansive.
- Jane Austen makes a general statement; Kendrick Lamar makes a reference to his own personal experiences.

6. In your opinion, which text does a superior job of communicating the author's main idea? Explain why (making sure to cite a piece of textual evidence to support your answer).

Possible replies; answers may vary.

Why Jane Austen's is superior	Why Kendrick Lamar's is superior
Jane Austen's brevity and directness make her words inspirational (and even quotable). She uses only 11 words to convey her thoughts.	Lamar is more expansive and brings in direct personal experience (in numerable lines) to add credibility to the motif he conveys that "pain can teach us much in a good way" (i.e., learned to love himself).

STUDENT WORKSHEET

Question: Is my cultural category my identity?

Consider the following two texts…

Text 1	Text 2
"Our scars make us know that our past was for real." —JANE AUSTEN	From the song "I" by KENDRICK LAMAR I wear my heart on my sleeve, let the runway start You know the miserable do love company What do you want from me and my scars? Everybody lack confidence, everybody lack confidence How many times my potential was anonymous? How many times the city making me promises? So I promise this I love myself

1. Identify a common theme that runs through the texts.

_____

_____

2. Cite a piece of textual evidence from Text 1 that supports the assertion you made above (in question #1).

_____

_____

3. Cite a piece of textual evidence from Text 2 that supports the assertion you made above (in question #1).

_____

_____

4. In what way are the authors similar in their approach to the subject matter?

_____

_____

5. In what way are the authors different in their approach to the subject matter?

_____

_____

6. In your opinion, which text does a superior job of communicating the author's main idea?
Explain why (making sure to cite a piece of textual evidence to support your answer).

_____

_____

OPEN MIC: PUTTING THE QUESTION TO YOU!

*Please answer the question below making sure that you
use textual evidence to support whatever claims(s) you assert.*

In your opinion, is violence an appropriate solution for resolving conflict?

_____

_____

_____

_____

_____

_____

_____

_____

_____

_____

_____

_____

_____

_____

_____

_____

_____

_____

_____

_____

_____

UNIT 7
APPLYING ARISTOTLE'S RHETORICAL TRIANGLE TO HIP-HOP

Making Claims and Supporting Them with Valid Reasoning and Meaningful Evidence

Essential Question

Who is the most influential hip-hop artist of all time?

Standards-Based Literacy Skills Targeted:

Identifying Common Themes Between Disparate Texts
Providing Textual Evidence to Support Assertions
Recognizing Compositional Similarities
Distinguishing Stylistic Differences
Rendering Opinions
Providing Evidence-Based Reasoning to Support Assertions
Reading Closely

Writing: Making Claims and Providing Evidence

APPLYING ARISTOTLE'S RHETORICAL TRIANGLE TO HIP-HOP
Making Claims and Supporting Them with Valid Reasoning and Meaningful Evidence

Aristotle was a Greek philosopher who divided the means of persuasion, appeals, and argumentation into three general categories: Ethos, Pathos, and Logos.

Ethos: Since audiences tend to believe people whom they respect and find credible, Aristotle maintained that ethos was an essential element of effective persuasion.

Questions to ask regarding ethos:
- What makes the person asserting the claim an authority worth listening to?
- Is he or she well informed, admirable, and worthy of respect?

Pathos: Appealing to an audience's emotions (i.e., winning the battle for their hearts) was another critical element Aristotle identified as an essential element of effective persuasion.

Questions to ask regarding pathos:
- Does the argument stir up strong feelings in the audience?
- What role does passion, anger, love, fear, and so on play in the claims being made, and how do these elements enhance the argument?

Logos: Using logic and valid reasoning to persuade an audience to buy in to an argument is also, according to Aristotle, essential to making successful claims. In fact, some scholars believe providing excellent logical reasoning is the true heart of argumentation and the most critical element in the art of persuasion.

Questions to ask regarding logos:
- What provable facts, statistics, and hard data have been provided?
- Are common sense, basic logic, and well-considered reasoning being presented to the audience in an organized and thoughtful manner?

Aristotle's Rhetorical Triangle

ETHOS
Credibility
Trust
Reputation

The Argument

PATHOS
Feelings
Emotion
Sentiment

LOGOS
Logic
Reasoning
Facts

The most influential group
of artists in hip-hop history is
Run-DMC

Who was the first rap group in history to have a #1 hit album on the charts?

Who was the first rap group in history to land a major endorsement deal?

Who was the first rap group in history to have an album go gold, to have an album go platinum, and to earn airplay on MTV (which was exclusively for pop and rock music videos at the time—with ZERO hip-hop in rotation on the station at all)?

That's right, Run-DMC. They were more than a musical group; Run-DMC irrevocably altered the entire musical landscape of a nation. They changed the sound of rap music, they pioneered a new style of street fashion and they brought the beats, power, beauty, and magic of hip-hop to pop culture across the globe in a way that shattered every glass ceiling that existed for hip-hop at the time.

All serious students of hip-hop acknowledge that Run-DMC were the primary artists to break down the final barriers that had previously prevented hip-hop from entering the musical mainstream, a feat which earned the group both popular and critical success. Their lists of first is INCREDIBLE:

- They were the first rappers to appear on *Saturday Night Live*.
- They were the first hip-hop artists featured on the cover of *Rolling Stone*.
- They were the first rap act nominated for a Grammy Award.

Prior to Run-DMC, rock-n-roll lived in an entirely different sphere than hip-hop. Then Run-DMC teamed up with the legendary rock band Aerosmith for the song *"Walk This Way"* and once they did hip-hop moved from the streets into suburbia—and hip-hop has never looked back!

Check out any list of rap's most influential artists from any of the most credible sources—from XXL to Vibe to the Rock-n-Roll Hall of Fame—and you'll see the name Run-DMC right up at the top.

There's no debate. At the end of the day when the rubber meets the road and the needle hits the record, it's clear that with so many firsts on their list of accomplishments, Run-DMC has demonstrated that they are the most influential group of artists in hip-hop history.

INTERPRETATION GUIDE
Making Claims and Supporting Them with Valid Reasoning and Meaningful Evidence

Assignment: After reading the argument that Run-DMC is the most influential group of artists in hip-hop history, complete the following:

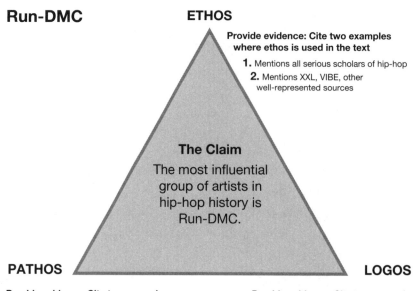

Run-DMC

ETHOS

Provide evidence: Cite two examples
where ethos is used in the text

1. Mentions all serious scholars of hip-hop

2. Mentions XXL, VIBE, other
well-represented sources

The Claim
The most influential
group of artists in
hip-hop history is
Run-DMC.

PATHOS

Provide evidence: Cite two examples
where pathos is used in the text

1. Putting the word INCREDIBLE
in all caps for extra energy

2. The rousing phrase, "There's no debate."

LOGOS

Provide evidence: Cite two examples
where logos is used in the text

1. Cites a variety of facts regarding
the firsts of Run-DMC

2. Gives a host of statistically
provable achievements

1. In your opinion, which area of Aristotle's Rhetorical Triangle is the strongest
(i.e., where was the author MOST convincing)?

_____ Ethos   _____ Pathos   ____ X ____ Logos

2. Explain why.

Logos is the strongest area because there are so many hard, provable facts given to back up the assertion that Run-DMC was the most influential hip-hop group in history.

3. In your opinion, which area of Aristotle's Rhetorical Triangle is the weakest
(i.e., where was the author LEAST convincing)?

_____ Ethos   ____ X ____ Pathos   _____ Logos

4. Explain why.

Pathos is the weakest area because an objective personal piece that doesn't show favoritism makes for a stronger argument. In this text, it's clear the author is a fan (and biased).

5. Cite one way in which the author's claim could have been improved.

The author's claim could have been improved by not making it seem as if the answer is so black and white. Other hip-hop artists have the right to be considered, but the tone of this piece makes it seem like it's not even a *question at all.*

STUDENT WORKSHEET
Making Claims and Supporting Them with Valid Reasoning and Meaningful Evidence

Assignment: After reading the argument that Run-DMC is the most influential group of artists in hip-hop history, complete the following:

Run-DMC

ETHOS

Provide evidence: Cite two examples
where ethos is used in the text

1. _____

2. _____

The Claim
The most influential
group of artists in
hip-hop history is
Run-DMC.

PATHOS

Provide evidence: Cite two examples
where pathos is used in the text

1. _____

2. _____

LOGOS

Provide evidence: Cite two examples
where logos is used in the text

1. _____

2. _____

1. In your opinion, which area of Aristotle's Rhetorical Triangle is the strongest
(i.e., where was the author MOST convincing)?

_____ Ethos   _____ Pathos   _____ Logos

2. Explain why.

_____

_____

3. In your opinion, which area of Aristotle's Rhetorical Triangle is the weakest
(i.e., where was the author LEAST convincing)?

_____ Ethos   _____ Pathos   _____ Logos

4. Explain why.

_____

_____

5. Cite one way in which the author's claim could have been improved.

_____

_____

The most influential group
of artists in hip-hop history is
Public Enemy

No one delivered a more thunderous blow to the fabric of hip-hop's evolving cultural identity than the group who boldly mixed intellectualism, politics and in-your-face confrontation with hard beats, complex rhymes and sophisticated musical arrangements. At a time when most rap artists were aiming for dance hits and blustery shows of braggadocio, Public Enemy was aiming to vanquish societal injustice.

And they sold millions of albums along the way.

Public Enemy raised a call-to-arms against bias, oppression, and tyranny through their music. Prior to Public Enemy's emergence, hip-hop was frequently dismissed by critics of the genre as a sexist, homophobic, lightweight, materialistic entertainment but this transformational group of musical artists showed how rap could be a vehicle for socially conscious political activism. As famed music critic Stephen Erlewine proclaimed, "P.E. brought in elements of *free jazz*, hard *funk*, even *musique concrète*, via [its] producing team the Bomb Squad, creating a dense, ferocious sound unlike anything that came before."

To the delight of fans across the globe, Public Enemy boldly produced sonically extreme sounds mixed with socially revolutionary politics that attacked highly-charged issues which plagued poor communities. Police brutality, inequitable education, crippling unemployment, Public Enemy shined a bright light on the ugly truth underneath all of these subjects and more. They were more than just musicians; Public Enemy were the original pioneers of politically charged rap, and the ripples of their breakthrough artistry still cascade across hip-hop's landscape today.

Of course, Public Enemy's innovative approaches didn't stop at simply calling attention to egregious disenfranchisement through hard beats and even harder rhymes. As businessmen, they changed the Internet's entire music distribution capability by being one of the first groups to release *MP3*-only albums. Activism and self-empowerment were not merely ideas others were supposed to embrace; Public Enemy walked the revolutionary walk themselves by putting millions of dollars of their own potential earnings on the line. Boldness screamed through the group's blood.

As the undisputed fathers of politically and socially conscious hip-hop, real game changers at the highest level, Public Enemy needs to be regarded as the most influential group of artists in hip-hop history.

INTERPRETATION GUIDE
Making Claims and Supporting Them with Valid Reasoning and Meaningful Evidence

Assignment: After reading the argument that Public Enemy is the most influential group of artists in hip-hop history, complete the following:

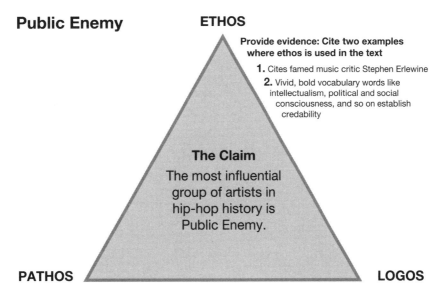

Public Enemy

ETHOS

Provide evidence: Cite two examples where ethos is used in the text

1. Cites famed music critic Stephen Erlewine
2. Vivid, bold vocabulary words like intellectualism, political and social consciousness, and so on establish credability

The Claim
The most influential group of artists in hip-hop history is Public Enemy.

PATHOS

Provide evidence: Cite two examples where pathos is used in the text

1. Appeals to emotions by portraying Public Enemy as a group that fought tyranny and injustice
2. Uses many dignified, admirable, positively charged words like pioneers, activists, innovators to describe P.E.

LOGOS

Provide evidence: Cite two examples where logos is used in the text

1. Cites data about selling millions of albums
2. Declares Public Enemy the fathers of politically and socially conscious hip-hop

1. In your opinion, which area of Aristotle's Rhetorical Triangle is the strongest (i.e., where was the author MOST convincing)?

_____ Ethos   _____ X _____ Pathos   _____ Logos

2. Explain why.

There are so many supercharged, powerful, positive vocabulary words singing the praises of Public Enemy's accomplishments that, in sum, they add up to a HUGE strength.

3. In your opinion, which area of Aristotle's Rhetorical Triangle is the weakest (i.e., where was the author LEAST convincing)?

_____ Ethos   _____ Pathos   _____ X _____ Logos

4. Explain why.

The piece does not provide an exceptional amount of actual data or statistics. It's mostly just opinion and strong feelings.

5. Cite one way in which the author's claim could have been improved.

The article could be improved by adding more measurable achievements to better support the claim. Statistics, tangible ways in which Public Enemy directly impacted hip-hop, more hard data.

STUDENT WORKSHEET
Making Claims and Supporting Them with Valid Reasoning and Meaningful Evidence

Assignment: After reading the argument that Public Enemy is the most influential group of artists in hip-hop history, complete the following:

Public Enemy

ETHOS

Provide evidence: Cite two examples
where ethos is used in the text

1. _____

2. _____

The Claim
The most influential
group of artists in
hip-hop history is
Public Enemy.

PATHOS

Provide evidence: Cite two examples
where pathos is used in the text

1. _____

2. _____

LOGOS

Provide evidence: Cite two examples
where logos is used in the text

1. _____

2. _____

1. In your opinion, which area of Aristotle's Rhetorical Triangle is the strongest
(i.e., where was the author MOST convincing)?

_____ Ethos   _____ Pathos   _____ Logos

2. Explain why.

_____

_____

3. In your opinion, which area of Aristotle's Rhetorical Triangle is the weakest
(i.e., where was the author LEAST convincing)?

_____ Ethos   _____ Pathos   _____ Logos

4. Explain why.

_____

_____

5. Cite one way in which the author's claim could have been improved.

_____

_____

The most influential artist in hip-hop history is
DJ Kool Herc

Many, many artists have contributed in many, many ways to hip-hop music and hip-hop culture but only one man actually invented hip-hop.

That man is DJ Kool Herc and because he was the very first there ever was he has to be considered the single most influential artist in hip-hop history.

Sure, people can talk about Jay-Z's entrepreneurialism. And yes, people can applaud Public Enemy's politically and socially conscious, game-changing music. Of course, there's no arguing that the group Run-DMC were the first to deliver international, mainstream popularity to the genre and that Queen Latifah broke through all sorts of barriers that existed for women who wanted to enter the hip-hop universe.

But did any of them actually invent hip-hop?

Think about it, none of these artists would even have careers if it were not for DJ Kool Herc. Without his brilliance, without his genius, without his creativity and innovation, there would have been no Tupac, no Biggie, no Drake, no Nicki Minaj, no Common, no Kanye, no Eminem, no Ice Cube, and on and on and on.

That's what makes him the most influential. When DJ Kool Herc started there was no such thing as hip-hop. Now, hip-hop is a multi-billion dollar cultural force that has done nothing less than change the entire landscape of music, fashion, dance, media and art. Hip-hop turned into a tsunami which swept across the entire planet. All because of one man.

Imagine if Thomas Edison never invented the light bulb? What if Alexander Graham Bell never invented the telephone? DJ Kool Herc is right up there on the Mount Rushmore of great inventors because, as everyone agrees, the Jamaican born DJ started hip-hop.

We know the date: August 11th, 1973.

We know the place: 1520 Sedgwick Avenue, Bronx, New York.

We know the musical breakthrough: Using two turntables for breakbeat DJ-ing

We know the vocal breakthrough: syncopated, spoken exhortations to the crowd now known as "rapping"

We know the man: DJ Kool Herc

How can there be any person who has made a more significant contribution in the whole history of hip-hop than that?

INTERPRETATION GUIDE
Making Claims and Supporting Them with Valid Reasoning and Meaningful Evidence

Assignment: After reading the argument that DJ Kool Herc is the most influential group of artists in hip-hop history, complete the following:

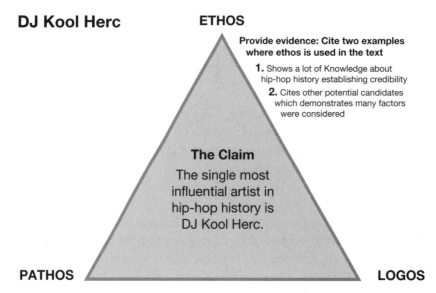

DJ Kool Herc

ETHOS

Provide evidence: Cite two examples where ethos is used in the text

1. Shows a lot of Knowledge about hip-hop history establishing credibility

2. Cites other potential candidates which demonstrates many factors were considered

The Claim
The single most influential artist in hip-hop history is DJ Kool Herc.

PATHOS

Provide evidence: Cite two examples where pathos is used in the text

1. Appeals to emotions by tying DJ Kool Herc to beloved and respected figures like Edison and Bell

2. Attributes all credit belonging to the efforts of one, innovative, creative, unequalled man

LOGOS

Provide evidence: Cite two examples where logos is used in the text

1. Cites specific data about dates, times, location, etc...

2. Declares that without DJ Herc none of the other people would have even excisted

1. In your opinion, which area of Aristotle's Rhetorical Triangle is the strongest (i.e., where was the author MOST convincing)?

_____ Ethos _____ Pathos _____ X _____ Logos

2. Explain why.

The strongest part of the argument is the specific knowledge of hip-hop history, which includes precise dates, locations, and people.

3. In your opinion, which area of Aristotle's Rhetorical Triangle is the weakest (i.e., where was the author LEAST convincing)?

_____ Ethos _____ X _____ Pathos _____ Logos

4. Explain why.

It goes a little bit overboard here with putting DJ Herc up there with some of the greatest rappers of all time. Throwing innovative dance parties and breaking through major scientific barriers that affect all of civilization are not necessarily in the same category.

5. Cite one way in which the author's claim could have been improved.

The author's claim could have been improved by not taking the *argument so far and making it seem as if everyone from Tupac to Jay-Z to Common and Ice Cube would never have achieved anything if not for DJ Kool Herc... that's a big stretch for these talented people.*

STUDENT WORKSHEET
Making Claims and Supporting Them with Valid Reasoning and Meaningful Evidence

Assignment: After reading the argument that DJ Kool Herc is the most influential group of artists in hip-hop history, complete the following:

DJ Kool Herc

ETHOS

Provide evidence: Cite two examples
where ethos is used in the text

1. _____

2. _____

The Claim

The single most
influential artist in
hip-hop history is
DJ Kool Herc.

PATHOS

Provide evidence: Cite two examples
where pathos is used in the text

1. _____

2. _____

LOGOS

Provide evidence: Cite two examples
where logos is used in the text

1. _____

2. _____

1. In your opinion, which area of Aristotle's Rhetorical Triangle is the strongest (i.e., where was the author MOST convincing)?

_____ Ethos   _____ Pathos   _____ Logos

2. Explain why.

_____

_____

3. In your opinion, which area of Aristotle's Rhetorical Triangle is the weakest (i.e., where was the author LEAST convincing)?

_____ Ethos   _____ Pathos   _____ Logos

4. Explain why.

_____

_____

5. Cite one way in which the author's claim could have been improved.

_____

_____

The most influential artist
in hip-hop history is
Jay-Z

Whether you know him as Shawn Carter, Jigga, or the husband of Beyoncé, Jay-Z is the most influential person in the history of hip-hop. With a life story that started in the projects of New York and reads like a timeless American rags to riches classic, Jay-Z has built a multi-dimensional, multi-national empire that is quite literally without rival.

Jay-Z didn't just break the mold; he invented new molds and broke them, too. It's like he once said: *I'm everywhere/ you ain't never there.* A brief overview of his accomplishments as an artist exemplifies a stunning musical career:

- Jay-Z holds the record for most #1 albums by a solo artist on the Billboard 200 (13)
- Jay-Z has sold more than 100 million records worldwide
- Jay-Z has received 19 Grammy Awards (and numerous other accolades).

The list goes on and on. In fact, many people consider Jay-Z the best lyricist in hip-hop to ever touch a microphone. The best! While many emcees only have one or two flow styles, Jay-Z has been called "The Master of All Flows" because he can do it all. Poetic. Syncopated. Fast. Slow. Straightforward. Narrative. Jay-Z is a rapper's rapper, a performer with diverse skills that many rappers tip their hat to and many others flat-out idolize.

Yet for all his success as a stage performer, some consider Jay-Z even more successful as a businessman working behind the scenes. For example:

- Jay-Z is the co-founder and CEO of Roc-A-Fella Records
- Jay-Z is the co-creator of the clothing line Roc-a-Wear
- Jay-Z is the former president of Def Jam Records, part owner of the NBA's Brooklyn Nets, a founder of the sports agency Roc Nation Sports, Co-Brand Director for Budweiser Select, co-owner of the 40/40 club, author of the bestselling book *Decoded,* and on and on.

Jay-Z is a rapper, entrepreneur, record producer, and one of the most financially successful hip-hop artists in history. Onstage, audiences across the globe find him to be an exceptionally dynamic performer, a true superstar, and he has sold out major venues like Madison Square Garden in record time. In the board room, executives find him to be an exceptionally shrewd businessman, a true superstar, and he's parlayed this combination of entrepreneurial and artistic acumen into a personal net worth of over $500 million (as estimated by Forbes).

From taking cover in the projects as a kid to landing on the cover of *TIME* as an adult, Jay-Z's career is unprecedented. There can only be one Number One most influential of all-time. That title belongs to Jay-Z.

INTERPRETATION GUIDE
Making Claims and Supporting Them with Valid Reasoning and Meaningful Evidence

Assignment: After reading the argument that Jay-Z is the most influential artist in hip-hop history, complete the following:

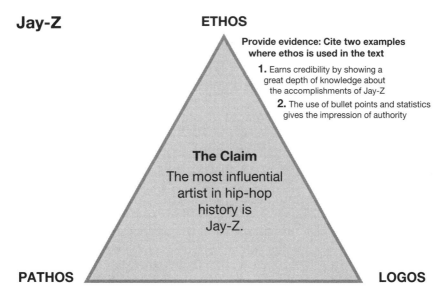

Jay-Z

ETHOS

Provide evidence: Cite two examples where ethos is used in the text

1. Earns credibility by showing a great depth of knowledge about the accomplishments of Jay-Z

2. The use of bullet points and statistics gives the impression of authority

The Claim
The most influential artist in hip-hop history is Jay-Z.

PATHOS

Provide evidence: Cite two examples where pathos is used in the text

1. Appeals to the emotions by making the declerative statement. "The best!" (note the exclamation point.)

2. Creates a real WOW factor by showing how Jay-Z rose from the projects of New York to becoming worth over $500 million

LOGOS

Provide evidence: Cite two examples where logos is used in the text

1. Cites an array of impressive facts about Jay-Z's accomplishments as a musical artist

2. Cites an array of impressive facts about Jay-Z's accomplishments as a businessman. (The combo is exceptional!)

1. In your opinion, which area of Aristotle's Rhetorical Triangle is the strongest (i.e., where was the author MOST convincing)?

_____ Ethos   _____ X _____ Pathos   _____ Logos

2. Explain why.
- The strongest area is pathos because the author puts together both the artistic accomplishments as well as the business accomplishments. Each of them alone would be phenomenal. Together, they are unreal!

3. In your opinion, which area of Aristotle's Rhetorical Triangle is the weakest (i.e., where was the author LEAST convincing)?

_____ Ethos   _____ Pathos   _____ X _____ Logos

4. Explain why.
- The author never really makes a logical case for the influence Jay-Z has had over hip-hop in general. Yes, he's been incredibly successful. But how has he "influenced" hip-hop? That information was not included.

5. Cite one way in which the author's claim could have been improved.
- If the author would have shown how Jay-Z changed hip-hop, how he took it in a new direction, how he directly altered the course of hip-hop history, then the argument would be improved.

STUDENT WORKSHEET
Making Claims and Supporting Them with Valid Reasoning and Meaningful Evidence

Assignment: After reading the argument that Jay-Z is the most influential artist in hip-hop history, complete the following:

Jay-Z

ETHOS

Provide evidence: Cite two examples
where ethos is used in the text

1. _____

2. _____

The Claim
The most influential
artist in hip-hop
history is
Jay-Z.

PATHOS

Provide evidence: Cite two examples
where pathos is used in the text

1. _____

2. _____

LOGOS

Provide evidence: Cite two examples
where logos is used in the text

1. _____

2. _____

1. In your opinion, which area of Aristotle's Rhetorical Triangle is the strongest
(i.e., where was the author MOST convincing)?

_____ Ethos   _____ Pathos   _____ Logos

2. Explain why.

_____

_____

3. In your opinion, which area of Aristotle's Rhetorical Triangle is the weakest
(i.e., where was the author LEAST convincing)?

_____ Ethos   _____ Pathos   _____ Logos

4. Explain why.

_____

_____

5. Cite one way in which the author's claim could have been improved.

_____

_____

The most influential artist
in hip-hop history is
Queen Latifah

How groundbreaking was Queen Latifah?

She became the first female rapper to be nominated for an Academy Award for her role in the film *Chicago*. She became the first female hip-hop artist honored with a star on the Hollywood Walk of Fame. She's the Chief Executive Officer of Flavor Unit Records, a successful company that has brought out highly acclaimed artists like Naughty by Nature.

As an actress, singer, MC, entrepreneur, and talk-show host, Queen Latifah has attained immense success across a variety of entertainment platforms and single handedly altered the manner in which every female in hip-hop now looks at their career. As friend and fellow recording artist MC Lyte said, "The Queen has no doubt changed the way the world views female MCs and their business potential."

Is more proof needed? Queen Latifah won a Grammy award for Best Rap Solo Performance. Queen Latifah's album *Black Reign*, a work characterized by socially conscious lyrics about female empowerment, went gold selling well more than 500,000 copies. Queen Latifa was also honored with the Sammy Davis Jr. Award for Entertainer of the Year at the Soul Train Music Awards.

Who else is a media mogul, a respected female MC and a COVERGIRL model? Who else even thought they could become all three and accomplish the feat with integrity and grace? When hip-hop was mired in many violent, well-publicized public feuds among various factions of rap performers, Queen Latifah refused to participate in the name-calling and negative interactions and instead spoke often about her feelings of solidarity with other rappers. While many others were picking fights, Queen Latifah stated she would rather present a united artistic front than negatively contribute to a hip-hop world fractured by infighting and clashing ambitions.

Queen Latifah is a role model who eagerly embraces her status as a person for other women and girls to look up to with enthusiasm and pride. It's her way of giving back and no one argues that the Queen paved the way for future female MCs like Lil' Kim, Eve and Nicki Minaj.

Queen Latifah invented the blueprint for successful female MCs/entrepreneurs and in a male dominated hip-hop world this was a tremendous feat. Undoubtedly, Queen Latifah must be considered the most influential hip-hop artist of all-time.

INTERPRETATION GUIDE
Making Claims and Supporting Them with Valid Reasoning and Meaningful Evidence

Assignment: After reading the argument that Queen Latifa is the most influential artist in hip-hop history, complete the following:

Queen Latifah

ETHOS

Provide evidence: Cite two examples where ethos is used in the text

1. Covers all the multiple dimensions of Queen Latifah's accomplishments in a way that shows deep knowledge

2. Speaks with authority and from a place that validates female empowerment

The Claim
The most influential artist in hip-hop history is Queen Latifah.

PATHOS

Provide evidence: Cite two examples where pathos is used in the text

1. Continually appeals to demales by talking about Queen Latifah being the first woman to do this and this and this

2. Accents all of the positive energy Queen Latifah brings to her career which shows how she is a woman to be admired

LOGOS

Provide evidence: Cite two examples where logos is used in the text

1. Cites a specific of facts regarding Queen Latifah's groundbreaking accomplishments

2. Points out specific places where she was the very first in hip-hop to attain many honors

1. In your opinion, which area of Aristotle's Rhetorical Triangle is the strongest (i.e., where was the author MOST convincing)?

_____ Ethos   _____ X _____ Pathos   _____ Logos

2. Explain why.
- In a male-dominated world, this piece shows how amazing Queen Latifah's groundbreaking accomplishments for females were in an excellent, passionate way.

3. In your opinion, which area of Aristotle's Rhetorical Triangle is the weakest (i.e., where was the author LEAST convincing)?

_____ X _____ Ethos   _____ Pathos   _____ Logos

4. Explain why.
- The argument is all about women, women, women, which is a good thing, but it represents only half of the world's population. To not admit this is a weakness.

5. Cite one way in which the author's claim could have been improved.
- The argument could have been strengthened by comparing how Queen Latifah measures up to the accomplishments of some of the most influential men in hip-hop. A groundbreaking woman does not make Queen Latifah the MOST influential of all time—it just makes her very influential and there's a big difference.

STUDENT WORKSHEET
Making Claims and Supporting them with Valid Reasoning and Meaningful Evidence

Assignment: After reading the argument that Queen Latifa is the most influential artist in hip-hop history, complete the following:

Queen Latifah

ETHOS

Provide evidence: Cite two examples where ethos is used in the text

1. _____

2. _____

The Claim

The most influential artist in hip-hop history is Queen Latifah.

PATHOS

Provide evidence: Cite two examples where pathos is used in the text

1. _____

2. _____

LOGOS

Provide evidence: Cite two examples where logos is used in the text

1. _____

2. _____

1. In your opinion, which area of Aristotle's Rhetorical Triangle is the weakest (i.e., where was the author MOST convincing)?

_____ Ethos   _____ Pathos   _____ Logos

2. Explain why.

_____

_____

3. In your opinion, which area of Aristotle's Rhetorical Triangle is the strongest (i.e., where was the author LEAST convincing)?

_____ Ethos   _____ Pathos   _____ Logos

4. Explain why.

_____

_____

5. Cite one way in which the author's claim could have been improved.

_____

_____

The most influential artist in hip-hop history is
Afrika Bambaataa

In order to properly identify who the most influential artist in hip-hop history would be, one has to look to the founding fathers of the musical and cultural movement. Just like America had Thomas Jefferson and John Adams, and Rock-n-Roll had Elvis Presley and The Beatles, hip-hop had its original visionaries who first lit the initial flame that became an international, multi-decade, multi-billion dollar forest fire.

Standing tallest among these pioneers is the man known as Afrika Bambaataa.

Afrika Bambaataa helped launch the careers of Fab Five Freddy, Run DMC, and the Rock Steady crew (among others). Afrika Bambaataa named hip-hop.

That's right, Afrika Bambaataa named hip-hop. At the time of its birth, there wasn't even a moniker for the new sounds and innovative scene starting to gesticulate in the South Bronx. So Afrika Bambaataa coined a term, something that would encompass not only the music, but the entire culture.

As celebrated hip-hop historian Jeff Chang notes in his book *Can't Stop Won't Stop*, "Afrika Bambaataa basically is The One," Chang says.

Afrika Bambaataa's charisma empowered him to rise to the rank of warlord in a local gang called the Black Spades but then he decided to turn a negative into a positive and use his influence to convert the Black Spades into a peaceful organization called the Zulu Nation in order to wage love, not war.

In a neighborhood characterized by poverty, crime and violence, Afrika Bambaataa had the credibility on the streets to proclaim hip-hop as a force for change and get even some of the most hardened residents to embrace his vision that hip-hop could be more than just music and parties and dancing but rather an actual cultural movement to effectuate positive change.

Though he only really had one "hit" as a recording artist—the revolutionary "Planet Rock"—the block parties where he'd preached the four elements of the hip-hop movement (deejaying, graffiti, emceeing, and b-boying (he later he added a fifth: knowledge)—laid the groundwork for all of hip-hop as we know it today.

Who is the most influential person in the history of hip-hop? Students of history know that the answer is clearly Afrika Bambaataa.

INTERPRETATION GUIDE
Making Claims and Supporting Them with Valid Reasoning and Meaningful Evidence

Assignment: After reading the argument that Afrika Bambaataa is the most influential artist in hip-hop history, complete the following:

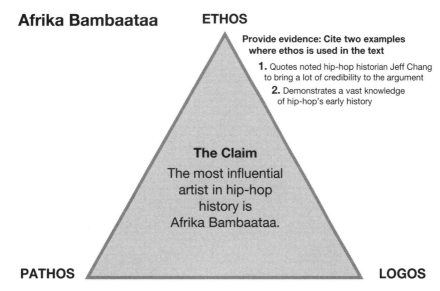

Afrika Bambaataa

ETHOS

Provide evidence: Cite two examples where ethos is used in the text

1. Quotes noted hip-hop historian Jeff Chang to bring a lot of credibility to the argument

2. Demonstrates a vast knowledge of hip-hop's early history

The Claim
The most influential artist in hip-hop history is Afrika Bambaataa.

PATHOS

Provide evidence: Cite two examples where pathos is used in the text

1. Appeals to the emotions by pointing out how Bambaataa turned a negative into a positive

2. Links Bambaataa to people like Thomas Jefferson, Elvis Presley, John Adams and The Beatles

LOGOS

Provide evidence: Cite two examples where logos is used in the text

1. Cites a variety of meaningful contributions that Bambaataa made

2. Clear reasoning with his argument that the man who named hip-hop is an unparalleled founding father

1. In your opinion, which area of Aristotle's Rhetorical Triangle is the strongest
(i.e., where was the author MOST convincing)?

_____ Ethos   _____ Pathos   _____ X _____ Logos

2. Explain why.
   ▪ The text cites a lot of specific, convincing evidence that shows how many pioneering elements Afrika Bambaataa contributed to the world of hip-hop.

3. In your opinion, which area of Aristotle's Rhetorical Triangle is the weakest
(i.e., where was the author LEAST convincing)?

_____ Ethos   _____ X _____ Pathos   _____ Logos

4. Explain why.
   ▪ The fact that Afrika Bambaataa never really made much music that became popular when so many other artists really broke through to mainstream and worldwide acceptance doesn't inspire an audience to believe he is number one of all time.

5. Cite one way in which the author's claim could have been improved.
   ▪ The author could have improved his claim by adding some quotes from Bambaataa about what it was really like to be a part of hip-hop's true beginnings.

STUDENT WORKSHEET
Making Claims and Supporting Them with Valid Reasoning and Meaningful Evidence

Assignment: After reading the argument that Afrika Bambaataa is the most influential artist in hip-hop history, complete the following:

Afrika Bambaataa

ETHOS

Provide evidence: Cite two examples
where ethos is used in the text

1. _____

2. _____

The Claim
The most influential
artist in hip-hop
history is
Afrika Bambaataa.

PATHOS

Provide evidence: Cite two examples
where pathos is used in the text

1. _____

2. _____

LOGOS

Provide evidence: Cite two examples
where logos is used in the text

1. _____

2. _____

1. In your opinion, which area of Aristotle's Rhetorical Triangle is the strongest
(i.e., where was the author MOST convincing)?

_____ Ethos _____ Pathos _____ Logos

2. Explain why.

_____

_____

3. In your opinion, which area of Aristotle's Rhetorical Triangle is the weakest
(i.e., where was the author LEAST convincing)?

_____ Ethos _____ Pathos _____ Logos

4. Explain why.

_____

_____

5. Cite one way in which the author's claim could have been improved.

_____

_____

The most influential artist in hip-hop history is

KRS-One.

by Adam Silverstein

KRS-One changed the direction of hip-hop forever by ushering in a new generation of emcees and becoming "The Teacha".

As a member of Boogie Down Productions, KRS-One introduced himself to the world in 1986 in one of the most famous underground hip-hop battles of all time. Representing the South Bronx, KRS-One and Scott LaRock went head-to-head with the more famous Juice Crew from Queens and decisively won the showdown. This victory propelled KRS-One into the limelight and emceeing has not been the same since.

Focusing on lyrics with a conscious message, KRS-One, along with artists like Public Enemy and Rakim, is largely responsible for bringing the "knowledge of self" dimension to hip-hop music and culture. He was also one of the first to see hip-hop as more than just a musical genre but rather an entire community. KRS-One pioneered the idea of tapping hip-hop's power to organize important cultural movements such as the *Stop The Violence Movement* in 1989 and *Human Education Against Lies (H.E.A.L.)* in 1991.

One look at KRS-One's impressive list of accomplishments further demonstrates why he must be considered one of the most influential hip-hop artists of all time. He's released over 20 albums in addition to having made hundreds of guest appearances on other performer's tracks. He's lectured at prestigious universities, authored multiple books, founded the Temple of Hip-Hop (TOHH) as a vehicle to teach and protect "Hiphop Kulture" (currently, the TOHH offers courses on how to become a hip-hop scholar) and even worked as a VP of A&R at a record company.

Not bad for a man who is indisputably recognized as one of the top emcees of all time.

Think about it. Who established the structure for hip-hop to be acknowledged as an international culture of peace and prosperity?

Who played a significant role in creating the "Hip-Hop Declaration of Peace", a document created to guide "Hip-Hop Kulture toward freedom from violence" and establish "advice and protection for the existence and development of the international hip-hop community and had it presented to The United Nations Educational, Scientific and Cultural Organization (UNESCO)?

Who authored *The Gospel of Hip Hop*, an 800 plus page manual that guides Hiphoppas in life and spirituality.

That's right, KRS-One. As the artist so eloquently put it, *"You are not doing hip-hop, you are hip-hop."*

His ability to see the bigger picture before anyone else as to the role that hip-hop culture would have on society and the manner by which he set a framework for hip-hop's positive growth to expand so that its highest ideals could be taught to future generations makes KRS-One the most influential hip-hop artist of all time.

INTERPRETATION GUIDE
Making Claims and Supporting Them with Valid Reasoning and Meaningful Evidence

Assignment: After reading the argument that KRS-One is the most influential artist in hip-hop history, complete the following:

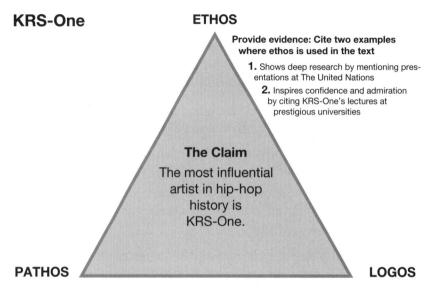

KRS-One

ETHOS

Provide evidence: Cite two examples where ethos is used in the text

1. Shows deep research by mentioning presentations at The United Nations

2. Inspires confidence and admiration by citing KRS-One's lectures at prestigious universities

The Claim
The most influential artist in hip-hop history is KRS-One.

PATHOS

Provide evidence: Cite two examples where pathos is used in the text

1. Says KRS-One is indisputably recognized as one of the greatest emcees of all time
2. The whole piece continually points to "positive" accomplishments in hip-hop

LOGOS

Provide evidence: Cite two examples where logos is used in the text

1. Cites a variety of facts regarding KRS-One's significant accomplishments
2. Points out all the movements with which KRS-One has been associated

1. In your opinion, which area of Aristotle's Rhetorical Triangle is the strongest (i.e., where was the author MOST convincing)?

   _____ Ethos   _____ X _____ Pathos   _____ Logos

2. Explain why.
   - The clear admiration for all of the positive cultural influences the author shows for KRS-One's contributions to the constructive power of hip-hop leaps off the page.

3. In your opinion, which area of Aristotle's Rhetorical Triangle is the weakest (i.e., where was the author LEAST convincing)?

   _____ X _____ Ethos   _____ Pathos   _____ Logos

4. Explain why.
   - While the author does a good job of showing his scope of knowledge, he doesn't give his credentials to weigh in as a hip-hop scholar.

5. Cite one way in which the author's claim could have been improved.
   - The author could have improved the claim by citing research that better supports his assertions about KRS-One's actual influence.

STUDENT WORKSHEET
Making Claims and Supporting Them with Valid Reasoning and Meaningful Evidence

Assignment: After reading the argument that KRS-One is the most influential artist in hip-hop history, complete the following:

KRS-One

ETHOS

Provide evidence: Cite two examples where ethos is used in the text

1. _____
2. _____

The Claim
The most influential artist in hip-hop history is KRS-One.

PATHOS

Provide evidence: Cite two examples where pathos is used in the text

1. _____
2. _____

LOGOS

Provide evidence: Cite two examples where logos is used in the text

1. _____
2. _____

1. In your opinion, which area of Aristotle's Rhetorical Triangle is the strongest (i.e., where was the author MOST convincing)?

_____ Ethos   _____ Pathos   _____ Logos

2. Explain why.

_____

_____

3. In your opinion, which area of Aristotle's Rhetorical Triangle is the weakest (i.e., where was the author LEAST convincing)?

_____ Ethos   _____ Pathos   _____ Logos

4. Explain why.

_____

_____

5. Cite one way in which the author's claim could have been improved.

_____

_____

Other Artists Deserving Consideration

Tupac Shakur

- Arguably hip-hop's most transcendent star.
- Sold over 75 million albums, and any list of all-time hip-hop "anthems" will include at least one Tupac song.
- Used his artistry to become the most recognized hip-hop voice for oppressed, impoverished people across the globe.

Grandmaster Flash and the Furious 5

- Pioneered the art of breakbeat deejaying (i.e., playing vinyl records and turntables as if they were musical instruments).
- One of the first rap "posses."
- Their album *The Message* was the first to demonstrate that rap could become a powerful and popular voice for the inner city.

Ice Cube

- A founding member of NWA, the group that brought gangsta rap to hip-hop and changed the genre forever.
- Produced cutting-edge social commentary that shattered the barriers of what the music and words of revolutionary music in hip-hop sounded like.
- Became a successful solo artist who evolved into an entrepreneur, movie star, film producer, and commercial pitchman while still retaining his hip-hop street cred.

Nas

- *Illmatic*, Nas's debut, is universally considered one of the best hip-hop albums of all time.
- Consistently listed as one of the top emcees of all time, Nas is thought to be hip-hop's most introspective rapper.
- Has six number one albums on the Billboard 200, tying him with Eminem and Kanye West for second-most of all time among rappers.

Lauryn Hill

- The first hip-hop artist to win five Grammy Awards.
- The first woman in music history to be nominated in ten Grammy categories in a single year (and the first woman to win five Grammy Awards).
- *The Miseducation of Lauryn Hill*, her first solo album, blazed unprecedented new trails for the entire genre of hip-hop.

Russell Simmons

- Founded Def Jam Records, hip-hop's first billion-dollar rap label.
- Was the behind-the-scenes businessman who brought out Run-DMC, Public Enemy, and a score of hip-hop's most influential and popular artists to the public.
- Despite becoming hip-hop's first mogul whose influence on hip-hop is undisputed, a question exists as to whether he can be considered an "artist."

PRE-WRITING WITH ARISTOTLE: USING THE RHETORICAL TRIANGLE TO MAKE CLAIMS AND SUPPORTING THEM WITH VALID REASONING AND MEANINGFUL EVIDENCE
Student Composition Preparation—Thinking Through Ideas

Assignment: Who is YOUR favorite hip-hop artist of all time? Complete the following:

Make YOUR Claim!

ETHOS

Provide evidence: Cite two examples where ethos is used in the text

1. _____

2. _____

The Claim
My favorite hip-hop artist (or group) of all time

_____

PATHOS

Provide evidence: Cite two examples where pathos is used in the text

1. _____

2. _____

LOGOS

Provide evidence: Cite two examples where logos is used in the text

1. _____

2. _____

1. In your opinion, which area of Aristotle's Rhetorical Triangle is the strongest (i.e., where are you MOST convincing)?

_____ Ethos   _____ Pathos   _____ Logos

2. Explain why.

_____

_____

3. In your opinion, which area of Aristotle's Rhetorical Triangle is the weakest (i.e., where are you LEAST convincing)?

_____ Ethos   _____ Pathos   _____ Logos

4. Explain why.

_____

_____

5. Cite one way you can improve your claim.

_____

_____

OPEN MIC: PUTTING THE QUESTION TO YOU!

Please answer the question below making sure that you
use textual evidence to support whatever claims(s) you assert.

In your opinion, is violence an appropriate solution for resolving conflict?

_____

_____

_____

_____

_____

_____

_____

_____

_____

_____

_____

_____

_____

_____

_____

_____

_____

_____

_____

_____

_____

_____

_____

_____

Glossary of Literary Terms

Alliteration	The repetition of the same or similar consonant sounds in words that are close together, for example, the sneaky, slippery snake.
Allusion	A reference to someone or something that is known from history, literature, religion, politics, sports, science, or some other branch of culture.
Context Clues	Using known vocabulary words that surround unknown vocabulary words to determine the unknown word's meaning.
Couplet	Two consecutive lines of poetry that work together.
Drawing Conclusions	Using cues from a text to figure out something that is not directly stated in the text.
Free Verse	Poetry that does not conform to a regular meter or rhyme scheme.
Haiku	Presents a vivid picture and the poet's impression, sometimes with suggestions of spiritual insight. The traditional haiku is three lines long: the first line is five syllables, the second line is seven syllables, and the third line is five syllables.
Hyperbole	A figure of speech that uses incredible exaggeration, or overstatement, for effect, for example, I could eat a thousand hamburgers right now.
Imagery	The use of language to evoke a picture or a concrete sensation of a person, a thing, a place, or an experience.
Inferring	Giving a logical guess based on the facts or evidence presented using prior knowledge to help "read between the lines."
Irony	In general, it is the difference between the way something appears and what is actually true (often incorporated for satirical effect).
Meaning	In general, it's what the text is about.
Metaphor	A figure of speech that makes a comparison between two unlike things without the use of like or as, for example, education is a life raft in the ocean of America.
Mood	The feeling created in the reader by the text.
Onomatopoeia	The use of a word whose sound imitates or suggests its meaning, for example, Boom! Smash! Pow! Pssst. Ssshh!
Pattern	In poetry, it's a combination of the organization of lines, rhyme schemes, stanzas, rhythm, and meter. (There are innumerable varieties in poetry.)

Personification   A figure of speech in which an object or animal is given human feelings, thoughts, or attitudes, for example, my computer stared at me, deciding if it wanted to cooperate.

Rereading   The act of returning to the text more than one time to "re-read" in order to make sense of and better comprehend a text (particularly a challenging text).

Rhyme/Rhyme Scheme   The repetition of vowel sounds in accented syllables and all succeeding syllables. The pattern of rhymes in a poem is called a rhyme scheme.

Rhythm   A rise and fall of the voice produced by the alternation of stressed and unstressed syllables in language.

Setting   The time and place of the action.

Simile   A figure of speech that makes an explicit comparison between two unlike things, using the words *like* or *as*, for example, my shoes were like falcons, enabling me to fly across the basketball court.

Sonnet   A fourteen-line lyric poem, usually written in rhymed iambic pentameter.

Speaker   The imaginary voice assumed by the writer of a text.

Stanza   A group of lines in a poem considered as a unit. Stanzas often function like paragraphs in prose. Each stanza states and develops a single main idea.

Summarizing   The act of organizing and restating the crux of the text.

Symbols   A person, place, thing, or event that has meaning in itself and that also stands for something more than itself, for example, the eagle is a bird, but it is also the symbol for American freedom, liberty, and justice.

Theme   The central message or insight into life revealed through the text.

Tone   The attitude a writer takes toward the subject of a work, the characters in it, or the audience.

Appendix: Authors, Artists, Rights, and Acknowledgments

- Abrams, Jim. "Congress examines hip-hop language." *USA Today,* 25 September 2007.
- Alexie, Sherman. The Absolutely True Diary of a Part-Time Indian. Little, Brown, 2009.
- Anzaldúa, Gloria E. "How to Tame a Wild Tongue." *Borderlands: La Frontera.* Aunt Lute Books, 2007.
- Austen, Jane. *Pride and Prejudice.* T. Eggerton/Whitehall, 1813.
- Bambaataa, Afrika. Universal Zulu Nation. 12 November 1974.
- Bambu. "Orosi" *One Rifle Per Family.* Beatrock Music, 2012.
- Big L. "Ebonics." *The Big Picture.* Rawkus, 2000.
- Blake, Emily. "Nicki Minaj Wants Out of the Female Rap Category." *MTV News,* 24 April 2014. Web.
- Chang, Jeff, Zirin, Dave. "Hip-Hop's E-Z Scapegoats." *The Nation,* 21 May 2007. Print.
- Cherian, Sharath. "Hip-Hop and Education—Educating Through Music." *Hip-HopDX,* 4 June 2014.
- Cole, J. "Love Youz." *2014 Forest Hills Drive.* Dreamville, Roc Nation, Columbia, 2014.
- Concepcion, Mariel. "The Billboard Q & A: David Banner." *Billboard Magazine,* 28 September 2007.
- Douglass, Frederick. "Rejoinder of Frederick Douglass and other black men to the President's speech." Washington Chronicle. 8 February 1866.
- Drake. "Dreams Money Can Buy." *Take Care.* Young Money, Cash Money, 2011.
- Duende. "Chicano Rap." *Revelation.* Aries Music, 2006.
- Dunn, Elizabeth, Gilbert, Daniel, Wilson, Timothy. "If money doesn't make you happy you probably aren't spending it right." *Journal of Consumer Psychology,* Vol. 21, Issue 2, April 2011.
- Dyson, Michael Eric, and others. "Versus Hip-Hop on Trial: Debate." *Google+, BBC,* 26 June 2012.
- Eminem. "Who Knew." *The Marshall Mathers LP.* Aftermath, Interscope, Shady, 2000.
- Hamann, Hilary Thayer. *Anthropology of an American Girl.* New York: Spiegel & Grau, 2010.
- Hazlitt, Henry. *Thinking as Science.* London: Kessinger Publishing, 2005.
- Hemingway, Ernest. "Notes on the Next War: A Serious Topical Letter." *Esquire Magazine.* September 1935. Print.
- Hill, Lauryn. "Final Hour." *The Miseducation of Lauryn Hill.* Ruffhouse, Columbia, 1998.
- Hitchens, Christopher. "The Perils of Identity Politics." *The Wall Street Journal,* 18 January 2008.
- hooks, bell. *We Real Cool: Black Men and Masculinity*. New York: Routledge, 2003.
- Hurt, Byron. "Hip-Hop: Beyond Beats and Rhymes." PBS, 2007.
- Ice Cube. "Counterpunch." *Los Angeles Times,* 25 June 1990.
- Immortal Technique. "Ultimas Palabras." *The Martyr.* Viper Records, 2007.
- Jay-Z. *Huffington Post*, 5 January 2015.
- Johnson, Lyndon B. "Remarks on the Signing of the Voting Rights Act." Washington, D.C., 1965.
- Kim, Seung Won. "Asian Americans Are Real Americans." *Iowa State Daily,* 5 November 2014.
- King Jr., Martin Luther. "I Have a Dream." Lincoln Memorial, Washington, D.C. 28 August 1963. Speech.
- Kweli, Talib. "Black Girl Pain." *The Beautiful Struggle.* Rawkus/Geffin, 2004.
- Lamar, Kendrick. "i." Single (album forthcoming). Top Dawg Entertainment, 2015.
- Litefoot. "My Land." *Good Day to Die.* Relativity/Red Vinyl, 1995.
- Malcolm X. "Ballot or Bullet speech." 29 March 1964.
- Mandela, Nelson. "An ideal for which I am prepared to die." Palace of Justice, Pretoria, South Africa. 20 April 1964. Speech.
- MC Jin. "Chinese New Year." *XIV:LIX.* The Great Company, 2014.
- Mos Def. "Hip-Hop." *Black on Both Sides,* Rawkus/Priority, 1999.

- Murphy, Tim. "Mississippi GOP Senate Candidate Blames Hip-Hop for Gun Violence." *Mother Jones,* 7 January 2014.
- Newton, Huey P. *Revolutionary Suicide.* New York: Random House, 1973. Print.
- Ortiz, Joell. "Latino." *The Brick: Bodega Chronicles.* Koch, 2007.
- Owen, James. "Modern Humans Came Out of Africa." *National Geographic,* 18 July 2007.
- Rakim, Eric B. "Paid in Full." *Paid in Full.* Island, 4th & B'way, 1987.
- Richburg, Chris. "Barack Obama Discusses Impact of Hip-Hop on Youth." *AllHipHop.Com,* 16 July 2007.
- Rohn, Jacob. "Lupe Fiasco Condemns Violent Lyrics in Music." *BET.com,* 25 March 2013.
- Ross, Howard J. *Everyday Bias.* Rowman & Littlefield, 2014.
- Sa-roc. "Black god theory." *Nebuchadnezzar. AVX Records,* 2014.
- Saba, Paul Ed. "Personal Reflections on the Asian National Movements." *Eastwind,* Vol. 1, No. 1, 1982.
- Salt-N-Pepa. "Aint Nothin But a She Thing." *Aint Nothin But a She Thing,* Polygram, 1995.
- Sandman, Homeboy. "Attack of the Clones: How Lack of Topical Diversity Is Killing Hip-Hop and Its Listeners." *The Huffington Post,* 3 October 2012. Web.
- Shakur, Tupac. "Violent." *2Pacalypse Now.* Interscope, 1991.
- Stern, Marlow. "Public Enemy's Chuck D on 25 Years, the Election, & Music Slavery." *The Daily Beast,* 19 October 2012.
- Stokes, Rachel, Garner, James. "How online collaboration transformed instruction at two schools." *eSchool News,* 29 October 2014. Web.
- Stone, Oliver. *Wall Street.* 20th Century Fox, 1987.
- Tall Paul. "Prayers in a Song." *I Don't Need Glove,* Soundcloud, 2013.
- The Lox, featuring Lil' Kim, DMX. "Money, Power & Respect." *Money, Power & Respect.* Badboy, 1998.
- "The O'Reilly Factor." Fox News Channel. 2 April 2002.
- The Roots, featuring Styles P & Mos Def. "Rising Down." *Rising Down.* Def Jam, 2008.
- Tindal, K. B. "Charli Baltimore talks female rappers." *Hip-Hop Vibe,* 6 August 2013. Web.
- Twain, Mark. *The Adventures of Tom Sawyer.* New York: P.F. Collier & Son Company, 1920.
- Walker, Alice. "The Gospel According to Shug." *The Temple of My Familiar.* Mariner Books, 2010.
- West, Kanye, Jay-Z. "Murder to Excellence." *Watch the Throne.* Roc-A-Fella, RocNation, Def Jam, 2011.
- Winfrey, Oprah. "Oprah Talks to Sonia Sotomayor." *O Magazine,* 28 January 2013.

Editorial Note: Legitimizing the credibility and illuminating the literary merit of the aforementioned artists by validating their work as being worthy of thoughtful academic discussion in a standards-based, rigor-driven classroom is a productive, transformational means of analysis by which the artists benefit. Of course, by shining a scholastic light on these materials and viewing all content through the lens of academia for the purpose of teaching and education, we also aim to drive greater sales for all of the artists included in this text, and **we strongly encourage all readers to purchase the full iteration of the included works.** *While the transformative nature of the usage herein adds something new to the original material—with a further purpose and different character that significantly yet definitely alter the work by means of a new expression, meaning, or message—we also aim to raise awareness about the extremely small and highly selective slices of literary excellence being demonstrated by the artists by providing publicity for their work in arenas that have not traditionally recognized these artists' scholarly merit. Additionally, by transforming the character, meaning, or message of the original as we have toward a socially productive use (i.e., creating a transformative tool to better educate underachieving, low-performing, disengaged students from primarily low socioeconomic backgrounds who can use the vehicle of becoming better educated to hoist themselves out of highly disadvantageous social ruts such as poverty, disenfranchisement, illiteracy, and so on), all artistic exemplars have been selected based on their ability to serve the new purpose of academic, standards-based literary studies.*

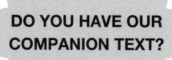